THE BIBLE
AND
SCIENCE:

Are They In Conflict?

What Does the Bible
Say About Science?

By
Don Stewart

The Bible and Science:
Are They in Conflict?

By Don Stewart

© 1993 By Don Stewart

Published by
AusAmerica Publishers
Box 28010
Spokane, Washington 99228

ISBN 1-877825-04-2

PRINTED IN MALAYSIA

All Scripture quotations are from the *New King James Version* unless otherwise noted.

Table Of Contents

Introduction

Introduction

Is the universe a result of chance or design? Did mankind evolve from apes or was he made in God's image? Does the Bible speak with authority concerning science? Over the years I have been asked many such questions regarding the Bible and its relationship to science. The need for a book on the subject became obvious.

Introductory Work

This book is a primer. Its purpose is to introduce people to what the Bible has to say concerning matters of science. It has not been written to trained scientists or specialists but rather to interested laymen who wish to know the biblical position concerning scientific issues. Neither is it the purpose of this volume to give detailed scientific arguments. That has already been well-done by others. A recommended reading list has been prepared for those who wish to pursue the scientific matters further.

Importance

From the first page until the last, the Bible records events which touch upon the realm of science and nature. The Book of Genesis records a supernatural creation of the world. The remainder of the Bible chronicles God's dealings with mankind, including miraculous events that break the so-called laws of science. It is important to understand how these events should be interpreted.

Today the theory of chance evolution is widely believed to have been proven true. Why, one may ask, should a person consult the Bible regarding a scientific theory? The reason is that the theory of evolution is more than a mere scientific theory. It is an all-encompassing belief system about the history of the origin and development of life on this planet. The theory of evolution is concerned with events about which the Bible speaks. We have the right, therefore, to question this theory and compare it with what the Bible says. The conclusions we draw will explain who we are as humans, the meaning of our existence, and our ultimate destiny. The issues could not be more important.

Scope Of The Study

The book will take the reader through introductory matters pertaining to the Bible and science. The first section will deal with questions such as: Are we here by chance or design? What answers can science provide us? Why should the Bible be consulted regarding areas of science?

The second part will deal with the subject of origins. We will discuss different views concerning how the universe and life itself originated. We will stress the fact that it is seemingly impossible that life could have arisen by mere chance.

Part three spells out the creation/evolution conflict. It will be shown that these two theories are in complete conflict with each other with no possibility of reconciling them. The compromising view of theistic evolution will also be discussed.

The fourth section will deal with scientific difficulties found in Scripture. Whenever the subject of the Bible and science is addressed, questions such as Joshua's long day and Jonah and the fish are usually brought up. If the Bible is scientifically accurate these and other questions need to be explained.

The last section will conclude that the Bible and science are not in conflict by showing that the Scriptures were far ahead of their time in areas pertaining to science. We will also stress that satisfying answers to questions of our existence and purpose for living can only be found in the Bible.

Right To Believe

Though most of us would not qualify as experts in any scientific field, we still have a right to hold our beliefs. Scientist Donald Chittick writes:

A young student needs to remember that he has as much right to believe as the oldest man on earth. Even though those around him may be applying tremendous pressure for a different interpretation, and even though the student may not yet be an expert, he can still be a good student while he remembers that ultimate truth does not come from 'experts.' Ultimate truth comes from The Expert (Donald Chittick, *The Controversy*, Portland: Multnomah Press, 1983, p. 45).

No Final Conflict

As we shall see in this volume, there is no ultimate conflict between a reasonable interpretation of science and a reasonable interpretation of the Bible. If the God of the Bible is the Creator of the universe then the Book of Scripture should tell the same story as the Book of Nature. The evidence will reveal that it does.

Introductory Topics

In the beginning God created the heavens and the earth
(Genesis 1:1).

1

ARE WE HERE BY
CHANCE OR DESIGN?

As we begin to examine the subject of the Bible and its relationship to modern unbelieving science, the central issue before us concerns our identity as human beings. Is our universe the result of blind chance or has it been supernaturally formed by a Creator? Is humanity the product of a series of fortunate, accidental circumstances or have we been specially designed and created by an all-powerful God? Are we here by chance or design?

Two Basic Possibilities

There are two basic possibilities regarding the origin and development of life. Either life on earth was supernaturally created by an all-powerful God or we are here as a result of blind chance. There is no realistic third possibility. Evolutionary scientist D. J. Futuyma writes:

Creation and evolution, between them exhaust the possible explanations for the origin of living things. Organisms either appeared on the earth fully developed or they did not. If they did not, they must have developed from pre-existing species by some process of modification. If they did appear in a fully developed state, they must have been created by some omnipotent intelligence (D. J. Futuyma, *Science on Trial,* New York: Pantheon Books, 1983, p. 197).

The theory of evolution holds that life arose by a series of chance happenings without any intervention by God. Life is still developing from simple forms to more complex ones. The following is a typical way the theory is described:

Living creatures on earth are a direct product of the earth. There is now little doubt that living things owe their origin entirely to certain physical and chemical properties of the ancient earth. Nothing supernatural was involved—only time and natural physical and chemical laws operating with the peculiarly suitable earthly environment (Paul B. Weisz, *The Science of Biology,* New York: McGraw-Hill, 1959, p. 21).

Created By God

The Bible, on the other hand, says that mankind and the universe were created by an infinite personal God. God designed and created the universe out of nothing. The Bible says God has finished creating and the universe is now complete. Nothing new is being created.

The biblical doctrine of supernatural creation and the modern atheistic theory of evolution cannot be harmonized because they teach two totally different views about our origin. It is a choice between mindless chance and intelligent design.

Apart from biblical teaching of special creation and atheistic evolution, there are two other views that attempt to explain the origin and development of the universe: (1) theistic evolution and (2) creation by some unknown Life-Force.

God And Evolution

There are some Christians who opt for a middle ground where God used chance evolutionary methods to bring about life as we know it. This is known as theistic evolution. One Old Testament scholar has written:

Is it possible to be a theist and accept the theory of evolution? Yes. The options are rather to be a theistic evolutionist or an atheistic one. In either case, evolution stays (Mark Hillmer, *The Genesis Debate*, Ronald Youngblood Ed., Nashville: Thomas Nelson Publishers, 1986, p. 106).

Unfortunately, theistic evolution fits neither the Bible nor science in its attempt to find a middle ground between the two. Darwin made it clear that the supernatural was unnecessary in his theory. The Bible excludes naturalistic evolution. Theistic evolution tries to ride two horses, creation and evolution, which are going in opposite directions. A thorough study of Scripture will find the two ideas impossible to harmonize (we consider the issue of theistic evolution in detail in question 20).

Life-Force

There are some individuals who reject evolution yet do not want to accept the ideal of a personal Creator-God. They attribute the universe as the creation of some unknown Life-Force. The idea of a Life-Force has an impersonal god or Mind creating the universe and then backing off from its initial creation. This view has gained favor with those who feel the need to maintain that creation was the work of some Life-Force but do not want to have to answer to this entity. C. S. Lewis calls this idea "Creative Evolution":

One reason why many people find Creative Evolution so attractive is that it gives one much of the emotional comfort of believing in God and none of the less pleasant consequences. When you are feeling fit and the sun is shining and you do not want to believe that the whole universe is a mere mechanical dance of atoms, it is nice to be able to think of this great mysterious Force rolling on through the centuries and carrying you on its crest. If, on the other hand, you want to do something rather shabby, the Life-Force, being only a blind force, with no morals and no mind, will never interfere with you like that troublesome God we learned about when we were children. The Life-Force is a sort of tame God. You can switch it on when you want, but it will not bother you. All the thrills of religion and none of the cost. Is the Life-Force the greatest achievement of wishful thinking the world has yet seen? (C. S. Lewis, *Mere Christianity*, New York: MacMillan, 1965, p. 35).

Just who or what this "Mind" is we do not know because it has not bothered to reveal itself to us. We do not know if it is one god or a series of gods. Consequently, it is of no help in sorting out the ultimate questions of our existence.

Furthermore, an unknown impersonal Life-Force cannot adequately explain the world as we know it. If mankind is the creation of some impersonal Life-Force why do we have personality? Why do such things as love, hate, and personality exist? An impersonal Life-Force cannot account for these things.

Both Explanations Inadequate

Theistic evolution and the Life-Force theory attempt to avoid the conflict between biblical creationism and naturalistic evolution. They are both inadequate explanations to the question of our origin and development. In this book, therefore, we will concentrate on the biblical outlook and compare it to the popular theory of chance evolution.

Summary

The modern atheistic theory of evolution and the biblical teaching of special creation are the two basic ways that we can view the origin and development of life. Compromise suggestions such as theistic evolution or the Life-Force theory are inadequate explanations.

Are we here by God's supernatural design or are we a product of mindless chance? The answer to this question is the focus of the rest of this book.

2

WHAT ANSWERS CAN SCIENCE PROVIDE HUMANITY?

Why did life on earth begin? Why are we here? What is our purpose for existence? Is there an Intelligence who designed the universe, or is everything the result of chance? If an Intelligence did create the universe who is He?

Unfortunately, science can never really answer the above questions. It can only describe our universe and the way in which it regularly operates. Science, as we shall see, is limited in what it can tell us.

Cannot Observe Past

One limitation of science is that it cannot directly observe the past. Scientists study the earth as it exists *today*. Scientists who make observations through a microscope or a telescope record our universe as it presently stands. Science can gather evidence about the past but it cannot prove what happened. This is because science relies on *repeatable* verification. The scientific method requires multiple, direct or indirect observations of repeatable events. The scientist in the laboratory does his experiment today and expects to be able to do it again tomorrow with the same results. Since any conclusion regarding past events or circumstances cannot be made as a result of direct observation or experimentation, it places them outside the realm of "scientific proof."

Beyond Scientific Inquiry

No question about our origins can be answered scientifically because first origin questions involve events that are forever in the past. The very beginnings of the universe, and of life on earth, cannot be repeated. Neither was there any human to observe and record them. Hence, questions about the origin of life and the universe are unable to be considered by the scientific method of experimentation and repetition. Scientist Robert Gange writes:

Events that are reproducible lend themselves to scientific inquiry. Events that are unpredictable lend themselves to statistical inquiry. But singular events lend themselves to legal inquiry. The creation of the world or of life are one-time happenings, thus lending themselves to such legal inquiry. The same, incidentally, can be said of the bodily resurrection that history records for Jesus Christ (a one-time happening). We must ask ourselves what role science can play in such questions.

Since science is concerned with reproducible events, it has no jurisdiction whatsoever in questions of origin or destiny. It can and does, however, gather evidence in support of one interpretation or another. In other words, it "assists the court" in gathering evidence on which the jury (you and I) renders a verdict. Unfortunately, we as jurists cannot be entirely objective because we are personally affected by the outcome (Robert Gange, *Origins and Destiny,* Dallas: Word Publishing, 1986, p. 33).

Any conclusion made on these subjects is ultimately based upon faith, not scientific proof.

Scientists Exercise Faith

This brings us to our next point—scientists exercise faith. Though the perception is often given that the evolutionary scientist deals with facts while the theologian operates on faith, this is not the case. The unbelieving scientist is just as much a person of faith as a believing scientist or a theologian. Agnostic scientist, Robert Jastrow, writes:

> Perhaps the appearance of life on the earth is a miracle. Scientists are reluctant to accept that view but their choices are limited. Either life was created on the Earth by the will of a being outside the grasp of scientific understanding, or it evolved on our planet spontaneously, through chemical reactions occurring in nonliving matter lying on the surface of the planet. The first theory places the question of the origin of life beyond the reach of scientific inquiry. It is a statement of faith in the power of a supreme being not subject to the laws of science. The second theory is also an act of faith. The act consists in assuming that the scientific view of the origin of life is correct, without having concrete evidence to support that belief (Robert Jastrow, "God's Creation," *Science Digest*, Special Spring Issue, 1980, p. 68).

Jastrow makes a couple of important points. There are only two alternatives a person has: (1) to believe in a Creator or (2) to believe that everything happened by chance. There are no other choices. Also, whatever a person assumes, he does so by faith. The explanation from both the creationist and evolutionist positions requires a person to exercise faith.

In the introduction of the 1971 edition of Darwin's *The Origin of Species* scientist L. H. Matthews wrote:

> The fact of evolution is the backbone of biology, and biology is thus in the peculiar position of being a science founded on an unproved theory—is it then a science or a faith? Belief in the theory of evolution is thus exactly parallel to belief in special creation—both are concepts which believers know to be true but neither, up to the present, has been capable of proof (L.H Matthews, *The Origin of Species*, by Charles Darwin, London: J.M. Dent and Sons, Ltd. , 1971, p. 10).

Scientist Ian Taylor also recognizes that those who take a naturalistic approach to origins must do it by faith.

While this naturalistic approach scorns the miraculous as an explanation, an element of miracle must nevertheless be involved since the mechanism for bringing order out of disorder is said to be chance. The alternative explanation recognizes that nature is ordered and highly complex, openly concluding that an intelligent Creator was responsible and that miracle was involved. In either case, each view is based upon faith, since there were no witnesses to our origins neither can they be repeated in a laboratory, they are essentially the unknowable and unprovable (Ian Taylor, *In the Minds of Men*, Revised Edition, Toronto: TFE Publishing, 1987, p. xviii).

Whether one believes life was supernaturally designed or evolved by blind chance, the belief is based upon faith, not repeatable scientific evidence or the testimony of a human observer.

Scientific Theories Change

It should also be noted that the history of science consists of one new theory after another. Sometimes theories are abandoned entirely. Other theories have been changed so often that they lose their original identity. They become like the proverbial pair of pants that ended up more patch than pants. There are times that a theory seems so factual that it is unchallenged for generations, only to be later overturned by the uncovering of new facts. Thus, a scientific hypothesis, theory, or law is not in the same realm as absolute truth.

Dr. Edward Teller, father of the hydrogen bomb, described the progress of science since the Second World War in the following way:

Practically everything that for years we believed to be true has been proven false or incorrect by subsequent discovery. In fact there is only one statement that I would now dare to make positively: There is absolutely nothing faster than the speed of light—maybe (*Readers Digest*, September 1970, p. 20).

Statements Must Be Challenged

Often in popular literature we read phrases such as "Scientists have proved that . . ." or "Science has shown . . ." or "Scientists believe . . . ."

These phrases are often used as insurance against any criticism of what is about to be said. If you can introduce a remark with "Science has shown . . ."or "Science has proved that . . ." then you can say almost anything and get away with it. However, no scientific statement is unassailable and no theory should be regarded as final.

Therefore, the so-called experts should be challenged as Marshall and Sandra Hall write:

> Who is to say, after all that ordinary citizens don't have the right to question any group of experts if that group's actions affect the entire spectrum of everybody's life, young, old, working or at leisure? If an engineer designs a bridge and it falls during the five o'clock rush and kills eighty-one nonengineers, who will say the victims' survivors can make no effective complaint because they are not engineers? If atomic scientists make some little slip and wipe out Oregon, are citizens from neighboring states to allow new atomic sites to be built near them because they feel unqualified as non-scientists in a making such a decision? (Marshall and Sandra Hall, *The Truth: God or Evolution*, Nutley, New Jersey: Craig Press, 1974, p. 99).

Scientists Not Always Objective

There is also the matter that scientists are human beings. The usual picture of a scientist is a person who is open-minded, willing to explore all areas and to study all the data. It is important to understand that there are some scientists who are not always detached, dispassionate observers. These scientists are not very quick to abandon their own particular theory even though they may find contradictory evidence. Only if all efforts fail and additional facts incompatible with the accepted theory are uncovered will they begin to consider other explanations.

Admission Of Prejudice

Some scientists have even admitted that they wanted to get rid of the idea of God as Creator. Aldous Huxley, one of the early advocates of the theory of evolution, wrote about his prejudices:

> I had motives for not wanting the world to have a meaning; consequently assumed that it had none and was able without any difficulty to find satisfying reasons for that assumption . . . The philosopher who finds no meaning in the world is not concerned exclusively with a problem in pure metaphysics, he is also concerned to prove that there is no valid reason why he personally should not do as he wants to do, or why his friends should not seize political power and govern in the way they find advantageous to themselves . . . .
>
> For myself as, no doubt, for most of my contemporaries, the philosophy of meaninglessness was essentially an instrument of liberation. The liberation we desired was simultaneously liberation from a certain system of morality. We objected to the morality because it interfered with our sexual freedom; we objected to the political and economic system because it was unjust. The supporters of these systems claimed that in some way they embodied the meaning (a Christian meaning, they insisted) of the world. There was one admirably simple method of confuting these people and at the same time justifying ourselves in our political and erotic revolt; we could deny that the world had any meaning whatsoever (Aldous Huxley, *Ends and Means*, New York: Harper & Brothers, 1937, pp. 312,315, 316).

Another scientific authority admitted that:

> Our faith in the idea of evolution depends upon our reluctance to accept the antagonistic doctrine of creation (Louis T. More, *The Dogma of Evolution*, Princeton: Princeton University Press, 1925, p. 20).

No Ultimate Answers

We cannot, therefore, look to science to provide us with any ultimate answers about our origin, purpose or destiny. The purpose of science is to describe the universe in which we live, but science can do no more than describe. Science can help us answer questions about *what* exists in our universe but it cannot answer questions of *why* they exist or *how* they came into existence. It is the job of science to observe the natural world and seek to understand it through that observation. Science can often say, "This happens," or "This is *how* such-and-such happens," but it is usually outside scientific jurisdiction to say, "This is *why* such-and-such happens." Unfortunately, scientists often overstep their domain and attempt to deliver declarations on subjects with which science, by definition, is unable to deal.

Science may unravel some of the mysteries of physical life, but it cannot address the question of right or wrong. The same science that can unlock the power of the atom cannot help us choose between good or evil ways of using that power. Therefore, terms such as good and evil, right and wrong, meaning and purpose, do not belong to the vocabulary of science.

Summary

Science attempts to give us knowledge of our universe but is limited in what it can tell us. Science can only observe our world in its present state; it cannot observe the past. Because past events cannot be repeated or tested experimentally, any theory about them is a faith assumption. Scientists, like the rest of us, exercise faith. Therefore, those who believe in chance evolution do so on the basis of faith, not indisputable evidence.

Finally, not all scientists have been objective in their dealing with the evidence. This should make us cautious about accepting a scientific conclusion too readily. Because of its limitations, and the fact that scientific theories continually change, science cannot provide the last word on any matter. Robert Jastrow offers a fitting observation:

Our theory of evolution has become . . . one which cannot be refuted by any possible observations. Every conceivable observation can be fitted into it. It is thus 'outside of empirical science' but not necessarily false. No one can think of a way in which to test it.

But now science comes to a great event—the birth of the Universe—and it asks: What Cause produced this effect? Who, or what, put the matter and energy into the Universe? Was the world created out of nothing or was it gathered together out of pre-existing materials? And: What force or forces created the outward momentum of the initial explosion? But that is just what science cannot find out (Dr. Robert Jastrow in a talk on "God and the Astronomers," Phi Beta Kappa Lecture, AAAS meeting, Washington, D.C., February 14, 1978).

Science is of no help in answering our ultimate concerns. Fortunately, the answers to these questions have been revealed to mankind by the Creator Himself. They are found in the pages of the Bible.

3

DOES THE BIBLE SPEAK WITH AUTHORITY CONCERNING SCIENCE?

In what sense should we look to the Bible as an authority on science? Should we seriously consider this ancient book to have the last word on questions of a scientific nature?

To many people the Bible is a book like any other book. It was written by men and is therefore fallible. It is argued, that any biblical reference about science, only reflects the unscientific and mythical view held at the time. Thus, the Bible is a book of human origin and its scientific statements are meaningless because they reflect the limitations of their times and are contradicted by modern science. Consequently, those who hold this view feel that modern science is free to go wherever it pleases without any reference to the Bible.

We Need God's Revelation

Does the Bible speak with the authority of the living God or is it merely a human production? From the first page until the last, the Bible claims to be the authoritative Word of God. It claims to have the last word on all matters of faith and practice. The Bible not only makes these claims but gives evidence to substantiate them (we have dealt with some of the evidence that the Bible is the Word of God in my book, *10 Reasons To Trust The Bible*, Spokane, Washington: AusAmerica Publishers, 1990).

If God exists, it is clear that humanity needs to hear from Him. The Bible says that God has revealed truth to human beings that we would not otherwise know. It is necessary that God speaks to us so we can know who He is and what He is like. The Bible says that God, "alone has immortality, dwelling in unapproachable light, whom no man has seen or can see" (1 Timothy 6:16).

God, by nature, is inaccessible to man. Therefore, we can only know as much about Him as He chooses to reveal. Without revelation we are only guessing when we speak about Him.

Testimony Of Jesus

The main reason Christians accept the Old and New Testaments as the Word of God is the testimony of Jesus Christ. Jesus claimed to be God the Son and backed up His claim with convincing evidence. If He is the One Whom He claimed to be then He has the last word on every matter.

As we survey the evidence we will discover that Jesus believed the Bible to be God's Word in both testaments. He taught that the Old Testament was God's Word and He "preapproved" the New Testament before it had been written.

1. Scripture

Jesus recognized the existence of Old Testament Scripture:

You search the Scriptures, for in them you think you have eternal life (John 5:39).

2. Word of God

Jesus said the Old Testament Scripture was the Word of God:

Why do you transgress the commandment of God because of your tradition? For God commanded, saying, 'Honor your father and your mother' (Matthew 15:3,4).

3. Unified

He also testified:

> The Scripture could not be broken (John 10:35).

4. Unalterable

Jesus also made it clear that the Old Testament could not have been altered, even in the slightest:

> For assuredly, I say to you, till heaven and earth pass away, one jot or one tittle will by no means pass from the law till all is fulfilled (Matthew 5:18).

Since Jesus demonstrated Himself to be the Son of God, His word on the matter is final. By definition, God knows everything and Jesus, being God, would know whether or not the Old Testament was His revelation to humanity. He made it clear that it was.

Therefore, we have the witness of Jesus Himself that the Old Testament was inspired by God.

New Testament

The New Testament is considered to be inspired of God for the following reasons:

Divine Origin

All throughout Jesus' ministry the divine origin of His words was stressed:

> He who rejects Me, and does not receive My words, has that which judges him—the word that I have spoken will judge him in the last day. For I have not spoken on My own authority; but the Father who sent Me gave Me a command, what I should say and what I should speak (John 12:48,49).

In addition, Jesus said His words would never pass away:

Heaven and earth will pass away, but My words will by no means pass away (Matthew 24:35).

That Jesus said His words would last forever hints at the idea they would be recorded.

Promise Of Jesus

The main reason we believe that the New Testament has been inspired of God is the promise of Jesus. Before His death and resurrection Jesus made the following promises to His disciples:

But the Helper, the Holy Spirit, whom the Father will send in My name, He will teach you all things that I said to you (John 14:26).

But when the Helper comes, whom I shall send to you from the Father, He will testify of Me. And you also will bear witness, because you have been with Me from the beginning (John 15:26,27).

We have two promises of Jesus contained in these verses:

1. The Holy Spirit would guide these disciples into all truth.

2. They would be given the gift of total recall of the things He said and did.

These promises look forward to a written body of truth. Those men to whom Jesus made these promises either wrote the books of the New Testament or had control over what writings were considered inspired. Since God had already demonstrated His desire to commit His Word to writing by giving His people the Old Testament, it would follow that He would do the same in a New Testament. The inspiration of the New Testament, therefore, was authenticated ahead of time.

Purpose

The purpose of Scripture is to call humanity into a relationship with God. The Bible says:

> And this is eternal life, that they may know You, the only true God, and Jesus Christ whom You have sent (John 17:3).

The Apostle Paul said that his goal was to know Jesus Christ. He said:

> that I may know Him and the power of His resurrection, and the fellowship of His sufferings, being conformed to His death (Philippians 3:10).

Divine revelation also reveals God's purpose for mankind. Only by divine revelation can we know who we are and what is the meaning of our existence. Divine revelation informs us that:

1. Man was created in the image of an infinite personal God (Genesis 1:26).

2. Man sinned and became separated from God (Genesis 3:1-24).

3. God became a man in the person of Jesus Christ and bridged the gap between Himself and man by His death on the cross (2 Corinthians 5:21).

4. Each individual is responsible before God and must personally receive Christ as his or her Savior (Romans 6:23).

Without divine revelation we would not know any of these things. Revelation is both necessary and reasonable. It is our only basis of speaking meaningfully about God. If the Bible is the Word of God then what it says about any subject should be taken seriously.

Conclusion

The Bible is unlike any other book—it is God's Word to humanity. Though the Bible was not dictated from heaven by God, it is a divine book. The human authors were led by the Holy Spirit with God supervising the writing of the original text. This includes the very words and phrases chosen. The Bible bears God's seal of truth in all its statements including those of a scientific nature. It is, therefore, the final authority on *all* matters about which it speaks.

4

HOW SHOULD BIBLICAL STATEMENTS CONCERNING SCIENCE AND NATURE BE UNDERSTOOD?

If the Bible is the Word of God then the question becomes one of interpretation. Though the Bible is the final authority on all matters, does the Scripture *intend* to give us any scientific information about the beginning and functioning of the universe? Did the biblical writers mean for us to take literally what they said in their statements about science and nature?

The following four theories have been brought forward by Christians to explain the Bible's relationship to science.

1. The Bible is God's Word to man but scientific statements are not to be understood literally. The purpose of Scripture is to bring mankind to salvation not to teach us about science. Hence, the Bible contains no useful scientific material.

2. The Bible is God's Word and does give us information about science. Yet the information is of such a general nature that it can be made to fit current scientific theories such as the theory of evolution.

3. The Bible is God's Word only in regard to theological statements. The only infallible statements in Scripture deal with spiritual matters (heaven, hell, salvation, sin, etc.). Statements of a scientific or historical nature, on the other hand, are not mistake-free.

4. The Bible is God's Word to man and the statements about science and nature are to be understood at face value. Though not a textbook on science, the Bible always speaks correctly when referring to scientific areas.

1. NO SCIENTIFIC INFORMATION

There are some Christians who believe that biblical references regarding science are not to be taken literally. They feel that it is not the purpose of Scripture to give its readers any scientific information. These interpreters view Scripture more as a theological statement where any hope of finding scientific information should be abandoned. The Bible, they say, should not be used to answer scientific questions about the age and historical unfolding of the earth. They maintain that Scripture tells us only that God is the Creator, but it does not tell us "when" or "how" He created. They view the opening chapters of Genesis as poetry, myth or allegory. Since any reference to science found in the Bible is not meant to be understood literally, the Scripture offers no useful and certainly no definitive scientific material.

This view, however, seems inconsistent with the facts of Scripture for several reasons.

Foundational Truth

The statements of Scripture that touch the areas of science and nature are written as history. There is no hint in the text that they should be interpreted as non-historical events. From the first page of the Bible until the last, these events are assumed to have literally happened. Furthermore, the truths taught in Genesis are foundational to the rest of Scripture. If one removes the first three chapters of Genesis from the area of fact, then the rest of the teaching of Scripture is meaningless.

Not Understood By People?

Often it is argued that the biblical writers as well as their audience would not have fully understood scientific references. Though this may have been true, it does not explain why they were given.

It is also important to note that the biblical writers did not always completely understand what they were recording. Prophetic messages, for example, went beyond the historical understanding of the people:

Although I heard, I did not understand. Then I said, "My lord, what shall be the end of these things?" (Daniel 12:8).

Scientific statements would inevitably exceed the current state of knowledge. It is not right to assume that the scientific statements had to have been completely comprehended by the people to whom they were originally given. God's revelation of Himself was for all time.

If the details of creation are not important then why are they recorded in Genesis and then restated elsewhere in the Bible? Why spend so much space telling us what happened if it did not occur in the manner in which it is stated?

Finally, we have examples of Scripture giving us science in advance (see Question 31). Though the giving of scientific truth is by no means the main purpose of Scripture, the fact that it is there should cause us to take it seriously. The idea, therefore, that the Bible contains no usable scientific information is incorrect.

2. MAKE THE BIBLE FIT (CONCORDISM)

There are many Christians who feel they must make the Bible correspond to the current scientific theories of the day. If the latest scientific theory calls for the universe to be ancient then the Bible will be found to teach it. If evolution is considered a scientific fact then the Bible will be made to teach evolution. Those who take this approach (called concordists) go first to modern scientific theory to determine what is true and then interpret the Bible in that light.

One such Christian writer says:

> We have to be willing to revise our interpretation of what the Bible means. We must acknowledge that we may not always have understood the meaning which the author intended to convey. Revising our interpretation of the Bible, however, does not demand a change in our estimate of its authority (Colin Chapman, *The Case For Christianity*, First American Edition, Grand Rapids: Eerdmans Publishing Company, 1981, p. 126).

Evolutionist T. H. Huxley sarcastically commented on the constant reinterpretation of Genesis by biblical scholars to fit current scientific theories:

> If we are to listen to many expositors . . . we must believe that what seems so clearly defined in Genesis . . . is not the meaning of the text at all . . . A person who is not a Hebrew scholar can only stand aside and admire the marvelous flexibility of a language which admits such diverse interpretations (T. H. Huxley, cited by Oswald Allis, *God Spake by Moses*, Philadelphia: Presbyterian and Reformed Publishing Company, 1943, p. 158).

Dangerous Consequences

Constant reinterpretation of the Scriptures to make it conform to modern science undermines the Bible's credibility. Scientist/theologian John Klotz perceptively summarizes the problem:

> Today creationists often find their bitterest opponents within the church. There are those who insist that theology must fit the Procrustean bed of science. The new god is science and therefore theology must adjust itself to the latest scientific findings. Too often the question in church circles is not, 'What do the Scriptures say?' but rather, 'How must we change our understanding of Scripture because of the latest scientific finds?'
> This is not to suggest that the approaches, findings, and research of the various academic disciplines are to be

ignored in understanding what the Scripture says. By no means. They have a role, and it is an important one. But it is a ministerial role, not a magisterial one. They are to help us understand the Scriptures; they are not to judge the Bible and its truthfulness (John Klotz, *Studies in Creation*, St. Louis: Concordia Publishing House, 1985, p. 87).

E.J. Young comments about Christians who believe the Bible must continually give way to changing science:

What strikes one immediately upon reading such a statement is the low estimate of the Bible which it entails. Whenever 'science' and the Bible are in conflict, it is always the Bible that, in one manner or another, must give way. We are not told that 'science' should correct its answers in light of Scripture. Always it is the other way around . . . on whatever subject the Bible speaks, whether it be creation, the making of the sun, the fall, the flood, man's redemption, it is authoritative and true. We are to think God's thoughts after Him, and His thoughts are expressed in the words of Scripture. When these thoughts have to do with the origin of man, we are to think them also. They alone must be our guide (E. J. Young, *Studies in Genesis One*, Grand Rapids: Baker Book House, 1975, pp. 53,54).

Double Revelation

If Christians make modern science more authoritative than Scripture the Bible is at the mercy of the latest finds of a changing science. Theologian John Whitcomb views the idea of making modern science more authoritative than Scripture as a double-revelation approach. He writes:

This theory maintains that God has given to man two revelations of truth, each of which is fully authoritative in its own realm: the revelation of God in Scripture and the revelation of God in nature . . . The theologian is the God-appointed interpreter of Scripture, and the scientist is the God-appointed interpreter of nature . . . whenever there is an apparent conflict between the conclusions of the scientists and the conclusions of the theologian . . . the theologian must rethink his interpretation of the Scriptures at these points in such a way as to bring the Bible into harmony with the general consensus of scientific opinion, since the Bible is not a textbook on science, and these problems overlap the territory in which science alone must give us the detailed and authoritative answers . . . After all, Genesis was written primarily to give answers to the questions, 'Who?' and 'Why?' Modern science, however, must answer the important questions, 'When?' and 'How?' (John Whitcomb, *The Origin of the Solar System*, Philadelphia: Presbyterian and Reformed Publishing Company, 1964, p. 8).

Whitcomb rightly chides those who hold to this 'double revelation' view of interpreting Scripture. Taking this approach reduces the authority of God's Word and places it in the hands of finite scientists.

Scripture cannot be continually changed to fit the present theories of science. Such an approach robs the Bible of its authority as well as casting doubts on its credibility. Scientific "truth" is limited and relative, while biblical truth is absolute.

3. LIMITED INERRANCY

Other Christians believe in a limited inerrancy of Scripture. They assert that the Bible is God's Word to mankind, yet they believe that it contains errors in areas of science, history and geography. The statements about God, heaven, hell, and salvation are supposedly error-free, but other statements contain mistakes.

This view of Scripture has obvious problems. If the biblical writers were mistaken in their historical, geographical and scientific references then why, one might ask, should their statements in the theological realm be trusted? It is meaningless to assert that the biblical writers made errors in history, science, and geography, but were kept error-free when they recorded statements in the theological realm (heaven, hell, salvation, etc.). We are asked to believe that statements that we can investigate (history, science, geography) contain some errors but statements that are beyond the realm of investigation (salvation, heaven, hell, etc.) are without error. This approach causes more problems than it solves. Francis Schaeffer writes:

> God has set the revelation of the Bible in history; He did not give it (as He could have done) in the form of a theological textbook. Having set the revelation in history, what sense would it make for God to give us a revelation in which the *history* was wrong? God has also set man in the universe which the Scriptures themselves say speaks of this God. What sense then would it make for God to give His revelation in a book that was wrong concerning the universe? The answer to both questions must be, 'No sense at all' (Francis Schaeffer, *The God Who is There*, Downers Grove, Illinois: InterVarsity Press, 1968, p. 92).

Textbook Of Modern Science?

A phrase that is often repeated is "the Bible is not a textbook of modern science." This is obvious. Nobody contends that the Bible could be used as a textbook for paleontology or biochemistry. Often, however, an illogical assumption accompanies this statement. Because the Bible was not written to teach science, some assume it may contain errors of fact about scientific matters. But this reasoning does not follow. The fact that the Bible was written mainly to communicate spiritual truth does not logically imply it contains errors of scientific fact. Joseph Dillow explains the sense in which the Bible *is* a textbook of modern science:

> In what sense, then, is the Bible a "textbook of modern science"? In this way: the Bible gives the modern scientist a framework within which to perform his research into the geophysics of the ancient earth. It provides a general framework and starting presuppositions for him. Since science in the purest sense deals only with that which is reproducible and measurable in the laboratory, when the scientist launches out in the question of earth history, he has taken a step of faith . . . The . . . assumption the scientist may begin with is that the Bible is true, and therefore what it teaches about creation, the age of the

earth, the Flood, and other scientifically related events is accurate (Joseph Dillow, *The Waters Above*, Chicago: The Moody Bible Institute of Chicago, 1981, p. 3).

4. UNDERSTOOD LITERALLY

We now come to the last of our possibilities. The view that makes sense biblically and scientifically is that the Bible does intend to give us factual information about areas pertaining to science and nature. The Bible, from beginning to end, contains a report of facts that are meant to be understood literally. This includes areas of science and nature. Either the creation account has a purely human origin and is meaningless, or it has been revealed by the Creator and is, therefore, binding on all of mankind. Theologian Kenny Barfield writes:

> Surely the being capable of producing the universe would understand the laws by which it was made. And any revelation from that being would also demonstrate a deep and almost prophetic comprehension of those universal laws we come to accept as "truth" . . .
>
> Although the Bible is obviously not meant to be a scientific textbook, any honest observer must admit that through the centuries the Bible has held a close, unchanging relationship to now-verifiable scientific principles. In addition, when the laws of science are reflected within its pages, they are presented correctly. Finally, when one understands the times in which the various books were written, that tie to truth becomes even more impressive (Kenny Barfield, *Why The Bible is Number 1*, Grand Rapids: Baker Book House, 1988, p. 9).

Bible scholar Eric Sauer makes an appropriate comment on this controversial matter:

> It is true that the main and real aim of the Biblical creation-narrative is of a thoroughly spiritual nature. All our efforts to understand it scientifically must never forget this. This applies to the whole of Scripture. We must agree with Augustine when he said, "We do not read in the Gospels that the Lord said, 'I will send you the Spirit, who

will teach you about the course of the sun and moon.' They were to become Christians, not astronomers." Nevertheless it cannot be denied that the first chapter of the Bible conveys its spiritual teachings in the form of a historical narrative. Unmistakably it affirms a series of acts of God following one on another and hence the progressive character of the process of creation. Therefore, just as we must not overlook the spiritual content of the creation story, we should also not despise what it contains regarding the history of creation (Eric Sauer, *The King of the Earth*, Palm Springs: Ronald N. Haynes Publishers, 1981, pp. 197,198).

Therefore it seems more consistent to let the Bible speak with authority on the areas of science that it touches rather than assuming the writers were only composing an allegory.

Non-Technical Language

It is important to understand that scientific truth is communicated in Scripture in non-technical language. Whenever any event occurs, there are two basic ways of explaining it. One way is to give a technical scientific explanation. Science has a language of its own, and events are often communicated in technical scientific language.

A second way of explaining things is to relate how the event appears to the observer. It is this non-technical way in which the Bible describes events that pertain to science and nature. For example, the events of creation recorded in the early chapters of Genesis are not described in terms of modern scientific classification, but are described from the vantage point of an observer.

The Bible does not use the technical language of science, but rather the language of the marketplace. The biblical writers dealing with concepts of their times used the language of their times. The scriptural language is the language of everyday use. The words of the Bible are neither scientific nor unscientific in nature, but rather *non*-scientific. The language of Scripture is the language of appearance. Biblical writers describe things as they appear.

Jesus taught in such a way that even a child could understand Him. God desires mankind to grasp truth and comprehend important things regardless of education, background, or IQ.

Not Technical Answers

In addition, the Bible does not attempt to give technical answers to technical questions. Since the Bible speaks in everyday language, it is not proper to look to it for answers explained in technical scientific language. Bernard Ramm writes:

> The Bible is a book for all peoples of all ages. Its terms with reference to Nature must be popular. Perhaps in the medical and nautical language of Luke there are some technical terms, but most of the vocabulary of the Bible with reference to nature is popular. It is therefore highly improbable for scientists to seek technical terminology in the Bible. It is also reprehensible for exegetes to try to find . . . references to modern scientific terminology in the Bible. The first is *unfair* in expecting a popular treatise to speak the language of science, and the second is *undiscerning* in making the Bible speak that which it does not propose to say (Bernard Ramm, *The Christian View of Science and Scripture*, Grand Rapids, Michigan, Eerdmans, 1954, p. 46).

In addition, literal interpretation allows for figures of speech. The Bible at times uses figures of speech to communicate its truth. If the Bible is read as other literature allowing the author to say what he wishes in the different literary forms, then there will be no major problem understanding that which is to be taken literally and that which is meant to be figurative.

God And Man

We again stress that the Bible was written chiefly with the relationship of man and God in view. According to Jesus, the central theme of the Old Testament is Himself:

You search the Scriptures, for in them you think you have eternal life; and these are they which testify of Me (John 5:39).

Likewise Paul's central theme was Christ. The primary purpose of the Scriptures is explained to us by the Apostle Paul:

And from childhood you have known the Holy Scriptures, which are able to make you wise for salvation through faith which is in Jesus Christ (2 Timothy 3:15).

The main purpose of the Bible is to make its readers wise for salvation.

Summary

The Scriptures are necessary to provide a philosophy of science for modern man. Award-winning scientist E. H. Andrews writes:

Is it possible for an ancient book such as the Bible to provide the Christian today with a philosophy of modern science? The answer given to this question . . . is a resounding 'Yes.' A biblical view of science is not only possible, but essential, if the church is refute effectively the largely materialistic outlook of our present age, an outlook that falsely claims the support of scientific evidence and knowledge. Without such a theology of science we are unable to relate spiritual truth to the scientific view of nature and thus by default we allow atheism to claim science as its own. To the ordinary man, science represents the objective truth about the real world in which he lives. Layman, though he be, he therefore tends to accept whatever world-view appears to command scientific respectability (E. H. Andrews, *God, Science, and Evolution*, Welwyn, Hertfordshire, England: Evangelical Press, 1980, p. 27).

God's Light

The Bible says:

In Your light, we see light (Psalm 36:9).

Christians must let the light of God's Word be the final determination of what is true and what is not. Scientific matters, when spoken of in Scripture, should be studied, not ignored. Furthermore, the Bible should be interpreted at face value without attempting to inject current scientific theories into it to make the Bible fit. It is a big mistake to surrender such matters as the origin of the universe and the beginning and development of life to the changing theories of modern science. The final authority for the believer must rest in God's revelation to us in Scripture.

5

WHY DO SOME SCIENTIFIC THEORIES CONTRADICT THE BIBLE?

As we examine the origin and development of the universe we will be discussing both modern science and the Bible. Though many times they will agree there are times they will not. The author of the Bible is the God of truth but scientists are not so infallible. Scientific *truth* can never contradict biblical truth but scientific *theories* do contradict the Bible in numerous ways. Why is this the case? If the Bible is God's Word and contains accurate science why do we find scientific theories at odds with Scripture?

Assumptions

The problem is not with the evidence that science discovers, rather it boils down to one's assumptions. All of us have our own biases and assumptions concerning the world around us. If a person assumes the theory of mindless evolution is true, then he will interpret the facts a different way than one who believes in divine creation. While all scientists deal with the same facts, the difference lies in the interpretation of the facts. The difference in interpretation can usually be traced back to the difference in assumptions.

Same Facts, Different Conclusions

,Two people who look at the same facts with different assumptions will come to different conclusions. We find an example of this in the New Testament when Jesus was speaking to the multitude. He said:

> 'Father, glorify Your name.' Then a voice came from heaven saying, 'I have both glorified it and will glorify it again.' Therefore the people who stood by and heard it said that it had thundered. Others said, 'An angel has spoken to Him' (John 12:28,29).

All the people had the same facts (hearing the voice of God the Father). Yet some would not believe what they clearly heard. They attributed it to thunder. Why? Because of their assumptions. They did not believe Jesus was the promised Messiah, therefore, they assumed God the Father would not approve of His ministry. When the Father spoke His approval of Jesus certain people *chose* not to believe it. The voice was not rejected because of the evidence; it was rejected because of their previous assumptions. This illustrates how people can have the same facts before them and come up with different interpretations of those facts based upon their assumptions.

Scientific theories fit into the same category. The assumptions the scientist brings to the data he discovers will influence the way the data is interpreted. *The difference lies not in the facts, but in the interpretation of the facts.* This is the reason why we have some scientific theories that contradict the Bible.

Wrong Interpretation

A further cause of the conflict lies with believers and their interpretation of the Bible. Sometimes the conflict between science and the Bible lies with a mistaken interpretation of Scripture. Theologian Eric Sauer notes:

> We must not *a priori* equate Scripture with our exposition of it. The so-called contradictions between faith in the Bible and science are in fact not a conflict between

the Bible and assured scientific knowledge, but between interpretations of the Bible and scientific theories; they offer a collision between popular traditions and philosophical speculations, which have been simply accepted from others without being tested (Eric Sauer, *The King of the Earth*, Palm Springs: Ronald N. Haynes Publishers, 1981, p. 202).

Christians must be careful not to assign blame to a scientific theory that contradicts Scripture until they are assured that their interpretation is what the Bible actually says.

No Contradiction

We emphasize that there is no contradiction between what is written in the Bible and the *evidence* of science. The Bible says,

Now faith is the substance of things hoped for, the evidence of things not seen (Hebrews 11:1).

Biblical faith is confirmed by the evidence we find in the world around us.

New Testament Message

The Apostle Paul defined the New Testament message as the death, burial, and resurrection of Jesus Christ.

Moreover, brethren, I declare to you the gospel which I preached to you, which also you received and in which you stand, by which also you are saved, if you hold fast that word which I preached to you—unless you believe in vain. For I delivered to you first of all that which I also received: Christ died for our sins according to the Scriptures, and that He was buried, and that He rose again the third day according to the Scriptures (1 Corinthians 15:1-4).

He declared that faith and evidence were so closely related that "if Christ is not risen, your faith is futile; you are still in your sins" (1 Corinthians 15:17).

The tomb was empty and many eyewitnesses testified that Jesus had risen. That was the consistent theme of the New Testament writers as they proclaimed the Christian message and intelligently defended their faith.

Evidence For Faith

In the first recorded message after the resurrection of Jesus Christ, the Apostle Peter based his argument upon objective evidence. He pointed to the world of reality to confirm the resurrection, appealing to the knowledge of his listeners:

> Men of Israel, hear these words: Jesus of Nazareth, a Man attested by God to you by miracles, wonders, and signs which God did through Him in your midst, as you yourselves also know . . . This Jesus God has raised up, of which we are all witnesses (Acts 2:22,32).

In his letter to believers, Peter emphasized the value of attesting evidence:

> For we did not follow cunningly devised fables when we made known to you the power and coming of our Lord Jesus Christ, but were eyewitnesses of His majesty (2 Peter 1:16).

He tells his readers that the evidence should cause them to believe in Jesus.

Written To Create Belief

The Apostle John, wrote his gospel for the purpose of creating belief:

> And truly Jesus did many other signs in the presence of His disciples, which are not written in this book; but these are written that you may believe that Jesus is the Christ, the Son of God, and that believing you might have life in His name (John 20:30,31).

John pointed to the visible signs performed by Jesus to substantiate that belief.

The Use Of Reason

The Apostle Paul emphasized the use of reason, evidence and common sense in testing and understanding reality. When Paul came to the synagogue of the Jews in Thessalonica, the Scripture records that,

Paul . . . went in to them, and for three Sabbaths reasoned with them from the Scriptures, explaining and demonstrating that the Christ had to suffer and rise again from the dead, and saying, 'This Jesus whom I preach to you is the Christ' (Acts 17:2,3).

The same chapter records Paul's dealings in Athens:

Now while Paul waited for them at Athens, his spirit was provoked within him when he saw that the city was given over to idols. Therefore he reasoned in the synagogue with the Jews and with the Gentile worshippers, and in the marketplace daily with those who happened to be there (Acts 17:16,17).

Scripture testifies that Christianity unites faith and evidence.

Bible Is Not Anti-Scientific

In addition, the Bible is not anti-scientific. Jesus Christ, for example, taught exact observation. In Luke 7:22 Jesus said, "Go tell John what you *see* and *hear*" (emphasis added).

The Gospel of John refers to testifying to what is known. The writer speaks of things, "which we *know* and *testify*" (John 3:31, emphasis added).

We are encouraged to observe nature. Jesus said, "*Look* at the birds of the air . . . *Consider* the lilies of the field" (Matthew 6:26,28, emphasis added).

John the Apostle wrote, "that which was from the beginning, which we have *heard*, which we have *seen* with our eyes, which we have *looked upon* . . . we declare to you" (1 John 1:1,3, emphasis added).

The early Christians based their faith upon what they knew, what they had heard and what they had seen.

Fits The Evidence

Finally, the biblical concept of God fits modern scientific evidence. Paul said:

> God, who made the world and everything in it, since He is Lord of heaven and earth, does not dwell in temples made with hands. Nor is He worshiped with men's hands, as though He needed anything since He gives life to all, breath, and all things (Acts 17:24,25).

The God of the Bible, the God proclaimed by and revealed fully in Jesus Christ, has a far better explanation of the origin of the universe than does modern unbelieving science. God "upholds all things by the word of His power" (Hebrews 1:3). This is the God who produced the universe and who sustains it today. He explains the *whys* and *hows* of our existence in the person of Jesus Christ.

Since the first explorations into space, our knowledge of the universe has multiplied a thousand times, yet we still cannot explain scientifically the origin of the universe. Living in an age of advanced science is not necessarily being closer to the truth of science. All secular theories are built upon an underlying philosophy: man is the master of his own fate, the captain of his own salvation, and is capable of being his own god.

The question of origins or the purpose of our existence is unanswered by the advanced, complicated, science of the twentieth century. It is the Bible, the Word of the living God, that provides answers to these questions. Scientific evidence, as we shall see, does not contradict the Bible. It does, in fact, support it.

Summary

It is not the facts of science that are in conflict with Scripture but rather the interpretation of the facts. Interpretations are based upon assumptions and the wrong assumptions can lead to the wrong conclusions. E.H. Andrews writes:

Scientific theories represent interpretations of the facts rather than the facts themselves. This distinction is frequently overlooked and historical evolution is presented as a *fact* rather than a particular interpretation of certain facts . . . There are alternative interpretations of these facts which are just as respectable scientifically as (some would claim, more so than) the theory of evolution (E.H. Andrews, *God, Science & Evolution*, Welwyn, Hertfordshire, England: Evangelical Press, 1980, pp. 89,90).

Christians can also be guilty of making the Bible say something that it does not. Therefore, we must strive to find a proper interpretation of both science and Scripture.

Long ago, Jesus pointed out the main reason for the conflict between the Bible and unbelieving science. He told the religious leaders of His day that they were ignorant of two basic things. He said, "You are mistaken, not knowing the Scriptures or the power of God" (Matthew 22:29).

A proper understanding of what the Scriptures actually say, and of the power of the God of the Bible, would go a long way to solve the apparent conflicts between science and the Bible.

6

HAS CHRISTIANITY OPPOSED THE ADVANCEMENT OF SCIENCE?

As we conclude our introductory questions on the Bible and science it is necessary to address a common misconception: Bible believers are opposed to the advancement of science. It is a popular perception that those who believe the Bible and what it says about matters of science and nature are enemies of truth and scientific advancement. The late science writer Isaac Asimov stated:

> With creation in the saddle American science will wither. We will raise a generation of ignoramuses. We will inevitably recede into the backwaters of civilization.

Three past incidents are usually cited to show the Christian's opposition to scientific advancement: the dispute of the church with Galileo, the creation/evolution debate between T.H. Huxley and Bishop Samuel Wilberforce, and the infamous Scopes monkey trial.

Galileo

At the time of Galileo, (the 17th century), the common belief was that the earth was center of our solar system. Galileo's use of the telescope brought conclusions that were based upon scientific observation. He taught that the sun, not the earth, was the immovable center of our solar system. This conclusion contradicted the accepted philosophical views of his day. But it is important to note, it did *not* contradict what the Bible had said about the matter. Scientist James Reid explains the arguments used against Galileo.

It would not be fair to consider Galileo's case without asking why the authorities of the day could use the Bible to support their arguments against him. The facts of the matter however, show that there weren't many Biblical references used. Galileo's enemies turned more to politics and the science of the day, than they did to the Bible. As indicated, they were worried more about upsetting the older "scientific" theories of the day (James Reid, *Does Science Confront the Bible*, Grand Rapids: Zondervan, 1971, pp. 44,45).

The church's mistreatment of Galileo gave the perception that Christianity was against scientific advancement and Galileo is hailed today as a scientific martyr. Yet the problem was not with the Bible and science. Arthur Koestler writes:

The Galileo affair was an isolated, and in fact quite untypical, episode in the history of the relations between science and theology . . . But its dramatic circumstances, magnified all our of proportion, created a popular belief that science stood for freedom, the Church for oppression of thought (Arthur Koestler, *The Sleepwalkers*, 1986 edition, London: Penguin Books, p. 533).

Huxley/Wilberforce

About a year after the publication of Charles Darwin's book *The Origin of Species*, a confrontation took place that set the stage for the modern creation/evolution controversy. In June

1860, at a meeting of the British Association for the Advancement of Science, a special meeting was held to discuss Darwin's views.

Bishop Samuel Wilberforce addressed the scientific association and spoke against the theory of evolution while English biologist T. H. Huxley defended Darwin. For the last hundred years the story has been told how Huxley won the debate against the ignorant bishop. But this view has been challenged in recent years. It seems the bishop was not the ignorant and ill-informed individual that history has usually characterized him. After the debate Wilberforce wrote a critique on the *Origin of Species* which Darwin himself described as "uncommonly clever' and which makes very good sense."

Because there were no written accounts taken at the meeting any descriptions we have are from memories of those who attended. The story that circulated was of Huxley's brilliance and the bishop's incompetence. Because of the way the incident was reported, many rejected the biblical position as being scientifically absurd. Within ten years, scientific opinion throughout the world had changed from supernatural creationism in favor of mindless evolution.

Scopes Trial

An incident occurred early in the twentieth century that furthered the rift between Christianity and the scientific community. In 1925 in Dayton, Tennessee, a young high school teacher named John Scopes was put on trial for teaching the theory of evolution. Scopes was defended by the famous Clarence Darrow while William Jennings Bryan argued the case for the state of Tennessee.

Evidence?

One of the pieces of evidence presented for the case for evolution was the tooth from Nebraska man. A molar found in Nebraska in 1922 was identified as having come from an important transitional form between man and his primate ancestors by at least four well-known scientists: H. Cook, H. F.

Osborn, H. H. Wilder, and G. E. Smith. Osborn declared, on the day he first saw the tooth:

The instant your package arrived I sat down with the tooth, in my window, and said to myself: 'It looks one hundred percent anthropoid' . . . It looks to me as if the first anthropoid ape of America has been found (cited by Bolton Davidheiser, *Evolution and Christian Faith*, Nutley, NJ: The Presbyterian and Reformed Publishing Company: 1969, p. 347).

However, in 1927 the molar was correctly identified as belonging to a pig:

The men from the museum also found more of the fossil material for which they were looking, and it turned out that the tooth of an animal which had previously been named *Prosthennops*. This was very embarrassing, because *Prosthennops* was a peccary, which is a type of pig (Davidheiser, *Evolution and Christian Faith*, p. 348).

Result

Unfortunately, Nebraska man was used as one of the "proofs" of evolution at the trial. Though the creationist position won in the courtroom, it was dealt a further blow in the eyes of the world. They perceived the church as persecuting a helpless biology teacher, as well as not accepting the clear evidence for evolution. Scientist Henry Morris sums up the result:

The bells had tolled for any scientific belief in special creation. The Scopes trial (1925) had ended in a nominal victory for the fundamentalists, with the teacher Scopes convicted for teaching evolution in the high school, contrary to Tennessee law. In the press, however, Clarence Darrow and his evolutionist colleagues had resoundingly defeated William Jennings Bryan and the creationists. Evolution henceforth was almost universally accepted as an established fact of modern science and special creation relegated to the limbo of curious beliefs of a former age

(Henry Morris, *The Troubled Waters of Evolution*, San Diego: Creation-Life Publishers, 1974, p. 9).

Modern Science And Christianity

These three instances have blurred the truth that modern science arose in a Christian context. Near the end of the nineteenth century, Emil Dubois-Reymond, professor of medicine at the University of Berlin, said:

Modern science, paradoxical as it may sound, has to thank Christianity for its origin (cited by Eric Sauer, *The King of the Earth*, Palm Springs: Ronald N. Haynes Publishers, 1981, p. 86).

Scientist/theologian John Klotz writes:

It should be very evident that modern science could only have developed in the environment of the Judeo-Christian emphasis on the orderliness of creation. The gods of the many religions are erratic. They play 'cat and mouse' games with man. They tantalize him and change the rules. Their actions are not predictable, and consequently the universe is not regular and predictable (John Klotz, *Studies in Creation*, St. Louis: Concordia Publishing House, 1985, p. 11).

The late Christian philosopher Francis Schaeffer concluded:

What we have to realize is that early modern science was started by those who lived in a consensus and setting of Christianity. A man like J. Robert Oppenheimer, for example, who was not a Christian, nevertheless understood this. He said that Christianity was needed to give birth to modern science ['On Science and Culture' *Encounter*, October 1962]. Christianity was necessary for the beginning of modern science for the simple reason that Christianity created a climate of thought which put men in a position to investigate the form of the universe . . . .

The early scientists also shared the outlook of Christianity in believing that there is a reasonable God, who has created a reasonable universe, and thus man, by use of his reason, could find out the universe's form (Francis Schaeffer, *Escape From Reason*, Downers Grove, Illinois: InterVarsity Press, 1968, pp. 30,31).

Summary

Because people took the Bible seriously modern science and its scientific laws were formed. The belief that a reasonable God had created a universe of order birthed modern science. Scientists such as Newton, Pascal, and Faraday were creationists who believed the Creator had established laws for people and the natural world. It is, therefore, incorrect to say that Christianity opposes the advancement of scientific knowledge.

Summary To Section One

As we have examined some of the introductory matters concerning the Bible and science we have discovered that the issues are very important. While the issue of science is not the main theme of the Bible, it still has important ramifications.

We have also seen that science has its limitations as to what it can and cannot do. It cannot answer ultimate questions about our existence. Because of its limitations we should be careful about overestimating its worth.

The Bible speaks of a Creator God who has made us in His image and likeness. Though there are some Christians who would ignore or water down what the Bible says about the creation and functioning of the universe, it is important to let the Scriptures have the last word on the matter. Otherwise, we are left to the authority of modern science and their constantly changing theories.

In addition, the Bible has provided the basis for modern scientific research. The belief in a God of order who created a reasonable universe gave mankind a reason to pursue scientific truth.

In our next section we will explore issues concerning the origin of the universe. Is there evidence that the universe came about by mere chance, or is there reason to believe that an Intelligence is behind its existence?

The Origin Of Life And The Universe

You shall not turn things upside down! Shall the potter be regarded as the clay; that the thing made should say of its maker, 'He did not make me;' or the thing formed say of Him who formed it, 'He has no understanding?'
(Isaiah 29:16)

7

WHERE DID THE UNIVERSE COME FROM?

Our universe is immense. Our own galaxy is one hundred thousand light years across and contains an estimated one hundred billion other stars besides the sun. Yet our galaxy is only one of a billion other known galaxies.

The origin of the universe has always been a source of mystery to mankind. Where did the universe come from? Has it always existed or did it come into existence at a certain point in time? If the universe is not eternal, what forces brought it into existence?

Although one might think that there are many possible theories as to the origin of the universe, there are actually only three. No matter which of the theories of origins a person chooses, any theory will fit into one of three possible categories. The three alternatives are:

1. The universe is eternal, although it may have changed form at various times.

2. The universe is not eternal. At a certain point it came into existence without any pre-existent cause.

3. The universe is not eternal but came into existence at a
    point in time, and was caused by something or someone
    other than itself.

The second or third possibilities are variations of the same
idea. Hence, we could narrow the possibilities to two: the
universe is either eternal or it is not eternal.

An Illusion?

Most people would laugh at the idea that the universe is
an illusion. However, there have been philosophers and
religious thinkers who have argued that all of existence as we
know it is some grand illusion. Others believe that the world in
which we live is not a real world after all. It is either a dream,
hallucination or thought in the mind of some god. Consequently,
they say that talk about the origin of the universe is ridiculous
since the universe doesn't really exist anyway.

If someone wishes to argue in this manner one can ask a few
simple questions. Does this person believe anything exists? If
he does, then what does he believe really exists (the world,
himself, etc.)? As soon as he tells us what he thinks is real,
then we ask him, "Where did that real existence come from?"
He is now faced with the same alternatives: either this real
thing has always existed, or it came about spontaneously with
no cause, or it was created by something or someone else outside
itself.

If a person continues to maintain that nothing actually
exists, then we don't have to talk to him at all, because he and
we, along with everything else, do not exist. Nobody is talking
to nobody about nothing.

1.   Is The Universe Eternal?

Most people who declare that the universe has always
existed do not actually believe that the universe was without a
beginning. Usually they say it is "eternal" because they cannot
imagine a time when the universe was not in existence. This
universe is the only dimension with which they are familiar
and it seems impossible to think of a time when everything
that now exists was not in existence.

There is new scientific evidence that the universe had a beginning. Scientist Robert Gange writes:

> There is another way that we know the universe had a beginning. Scientists routinely study the light from stars, which consists of waves that originate from the different materials that compose a star. Since the materials in the stars differ, the light waves that leave the stars and come to earth are different. The different light waves can be thought of as the material's fingerprint. Measurements of the light coming from the many stars show that the universe is made up of the same atomic particles that we find on earth.
>
> The Second Law of Thermodynamics, a law embracing physical things on earth, and the universe at large, governs how these materials can behave. Just a short time ago this law had limitations that prevented its application to the entire universe. But recently it was modified, and the revision (called the New Generalized Second Law of Thermodynamics) is vastly more powerful than the older Second Law.
>
> The New Generalized Law teaches that if the universe had been here forever, all of its materials would have reached a state of rest. But we do not see such when we study the universe with telescopes. And if the universe is not in a state of rest, it could not have been here forever, it must have had a beginning.
>
> The universe, therefore, had a beginning—a fact taught by the first verse of every Bible and now accepted by most of the scientific world. Every Bible begins with the statement: "In the beginning God created . . ." Now science says, "There was a beginning" (Robert Gange, *Origins and Destiny*, Dallas: Word Publishing, 1986, p. 16).

Therefore the idea that the universe is eternal is not supported by scientific fact.

2. Did The Universe Cause Itself?

This option maintains that something can come naturally from nothing—an idea that contradicts both science and the

Bible. One of the basic laws of science, the First Law of Thermodynamics, teaches matter/energy cannot be created or destroyed. Natural processes cannot bring something into existence from nothing.

What can we say to a person who believes that the universe just popped into existence from nothing? We can ask him to cite an instance of something coming from nothing. No such example can be found in the universe.

Furthermore, if this happened at the beginning of the universe there would be no reason why it should not happen now. But nobody seriously believes that things naturally just pop into existence from nothing.

Personal Or Impersonal?

If the universe had a beginning, as the evidence testifies, was it personal or impersonal. Was there some intelligence behind it, or did it just "happen" by chance? Christian philosopher Francis Schaeffer writes:

> An impersonal beginning raises two overwhelming problems which neither the East nor modern man has come near solving. First, there is no real explanation for the fact that the external world not only exists but has specific form . . . As I look at . . . the external universe, it is obviously not just a handful of pebbles thrown out there. What is there has form. If we assert the existence of the impersonal as the beginning of the universe, we simply have no explanation for this kind of situation.
>
> Second, and more important, if we begin with an impersonal universe, there is no explanation of personality. In a very real sense the question of questions for all generations—but overwhelmingly so for modern man—is 'Who am I?' For when I look at the 'I' that is me and then look around to those who face me and are also men, one thing is immediately obvious: Man has a mannishness. You find it today wherever you find man—not only in the men who live today, but in the artifacts of history. The assumption of an impersonal beginning can never adequately explain the personal beings we see around us, and when men try to explain man on the basis of an original

impersonal, man soon disappears (Francis Schaeffer, *Genesis In Space and Time,* Downers Grove, Illinois: InterVarsity Press, 1972, pp. 20,21).

3. The Universe Was Created

Though science and Scripture teach that something cannot come *naturally* out of nothing the Bible teaches that God *supernaturally* created the universe out of nothing. Scientific evidence also supports this fact. Robert Gange writes:

The First Law teaches that a natural process cannot bring into existence something out of nothing. If the First Law is correct, which seems to be the case, and if the universe had a beginning which seems to be scientifically accepted, then one conclusion is that something unnatural created the universe. If the world didn't result from a natural process, then it came about from an unnatural process.

The thought that the universe may have originated *supernaturally* is unsettling to many people. Yet, taken at face value, this conclusion is consistent with the total sum of evidence before us. Modern understanding of astrophysical data collected over the past fifty years or so has illuminated a profoundly important insight concerning the origin of our world. When objectively viewed, we see two complimentary truths: (1) Our world had a beginning, and (2) natural processes do not create things out of nothing. A supernatural birth satisfies them both (Robert Gange, *Origins and Destiny,* p. 18).

We are left with the alternative that makes sense both scientifically and biblically: the universe was created by something or someone outside itself. Christian scholar E.M. Blaiklock speaks of the challenge of accepting a created universe:

You can . . . believe, if you will, that the vision of order and interlocking purpose which we see all around us is a mere fortuitous congregation of atoms . . . the chances against the fortuitous formation of one protein molecule . . .

are beyond imagination. Such an event would require a volume of matter fantastically larger than the whole mass of the Einsteinian universe, with a radius, in fact, of 10^{82} light years, or, if the molecule envisaged is to be formed within that mass, it would require statistically 10^{243} billion years for the event. The figure baffles comprehension.

You may confidently tell me that any such chance event could happen before lunch, but I call to your remembrance that we speak of one protein molecule. How many millions compose my little finger, I do not know. If you will, you can . . . believe that an unimaginable complex array of atoms have produced the universe, the human person . . . hope, poetry, and beauty . . . but it seems to me that to accept such a basis on which to build your life and peace . . . you need a sturdier faith than mine when I chose to believe that a great Intelligence has ordered it all. Such a conclusion can certainly not be laughed away (E. M. Blaiklock, ed., *Why I Am Still A Christian*, Grand Rapids: Zondervan Publishing House, 1971, pp. 12,13).

Summary

The evidence points to the universe having a definite origin. The Second Law of Thermodynamics requires that orderly things inevitably break down and proceed in the direction of chaos, not the other way around. This fits the biblical model which says, "In the beginning God created the heavens and the earth." The universe had its maximum order and energy resources after creation and is now running down.

In addition, only the biblical model can explain the form of the universe, as well as the personality of man. Modern man has never been able to adequately answer these two questions.

8

IS THE BIG BANG THEORY
COMPATIBLE WITH
THE BIBLE?

It is not scientifically possible to study the origin of the universe. The experimental scientific method calls for testing and repeating a hypothesis. The beginning of the universe can neither be tested experimentally nor repeated. In addition, no human observer was present to witness the beginning. Despite this, various ideas or theories have been proposed on how the universe began.

Big Bang

The most popular idea regarding the origin of the universe is the big bang theory. Since the early 1920's, the majority of scientists have accepted the theory that the universe started with a big bang. The basic idea behind the big bang theory is that many billion years ago (variously estimated from 10 to 30 billion) all the matter in the universe was concentrated in a single point or sphere. At some point that condensed bundle of light (radiation) exploded with a big bang and the universe began to expand from that point. It is believed that mass, or solid matter, was formed out of the original radiation. After this explosion random chance took over. Molecules came together to form the various heavenly bodies. On earth non-living molecules came together to form simple life. Through millions of years this simple life evolved into the complex life we have today. This expanding of the universe is supposedly still going on.

The big bang model is based upon high speed computer models. These powerful computer models were made available by research that was necessary in the successful design of nuclear weapons during and after World War II.

Evidence Is Circumstantial

Evidence for the big bang is circumstantial. The main argument advanced for the big bang is the red shift of light spectra. The red shift might be a basis for believing that some aspects of the universe are expanding from some point of beginning. The problem is that no one can identify that point. Nobody knows from what point the universe is expanding, if in fact it is expanding.

Background radio noise and wave radiation, also offered as evidence for the big bang, might be a basis for asserting that remnants of some supposed initial explosion have been detected. It is also possible that exploding stars could be a basis for believing that if some parts of the universe explode, then maybe the entire universe resulted from an explosion. But all this is only inference. Astrophysicist Harold Slusher writes:

> The fact that the galaxies moving apart can be explained by many other states of matter and energy than a primeval atom that exploded. For that matter, the alleged explosion produces radiation and high-speed elementary particles, not galaxies. Galaxies moving apart have nothing whatever to do with the expanding motion of debris from an explosion (Harold Slusher, *The Origin of the Universe*, Revised edition, Box 2667, El Cajon, California: Institute for Creation Research, 1980, p. 24).

In addition, no one knows or can describe the initial conditions of the universe. Each of the points of circumstantial evidence may be used to support the idea that *some* beginning of the universe is required but not necessarily the "big bang."

Troubled Theory

Not all scientists are satisfied with the big bang theory. Astronomer Sir Fred Hoyle wrote:

As a result of this, the main efforts of investigators have been in papering over holes in the big bang theory, to build up an idea that has become ever more complex and cumbersome . . . I have little hesitation in saying that a sickly pall now hangs over the big bang theory. When a pattern of facts becomes set against a theory, experience shows that the theory rarely recovers (Sir Fred Hoyle, "The Big Bang Under Attack," *Science Digest* 92, May 1984, p. 84).

Scientist Lambert Dolphin notes:

Serious flaws [in the big bang theory] have begun to appear in recent years because of new evidence from the farthest reaches of space and new questions raised in nuclear physics (Lambert Dolphin, *Jesus: Lord of Space and Time*, Green Forest Arizona: New Leaf Press, 1988, p. 61).

Non-Christian scientist H. Alfven concurs:

On the other hand, there are an increasing number of observational facts that are difficult to reconcile in the Big-Bang hypothesis. The Big-Bang establishment very seldom mentions these, and when non-believers try to draw attention to them, the powerful establishment refuses to discuss them in a fair way . . . .

The present situation is characterized by rather desperate attempts to reconcile observations with the hypothesis to 'save the phenomena.' . . . In reality, with the possible exception of the microwave background condition, there is not a single prediction that has been confirmed (H. Alfven, "Cosmology: Myth or Science?", *Astrophysics and Astronomy*, 1984, pp. 79,90).

In the British journal *Nature* we find the following comment:

> Apart from being philosophically unacceptable, the Big Bang is an over-simple view of how the universe began, and is unlikely to survive the decade ahead . . . In all respects save that of convenience, this view of the origin of the universe is thoroughly unsatisfactory. It is an effect whose cause cannot be identified or even discussed (*Nature*, August 10, 1989).

Where Did Material Come From?

One problem not addressed by the big bang theory is where this material from the alleged big bang explosion originally came from. Scientist David Rosevear observes:

> Firstly one has to ask how the material in the universe arose in the first place. The first law of thermodynamics says that matter and energy cannot be created or destroyed. A theory has been advanced that, given the first few kilograms of matter, the rest could produce itself by a process of self-creation. Apparently this 'free meal' idea can be tolerated because, for such a unique situation, perhaps we should not expect the normal laws of physics to be obeyed! (David Rosevear, *Creation Science*, Chichester, England: New Wine Press, 1991, pp. 32,33).

Order From Disorder?

The big bang theory says that this great explosion caused order to increase in the universe. However, observation has demonstrated that explosions always decrease order, they are never known to increase it. The idea that some cosmic explosion could somehow generate a highly ordered and complex universe seems ridiculous to even consider. Since explosions generate disorder, this ultimate explosion would certainly have produced the ultimate in disorder. Yet astronomers continue to hypothesize that there was somehow inherent order in the "explosion."

David Rosevear notes:

The postulated big bang would have been the ultimate in destructive incidents. Yet we see our universe with its ordered spiral galaxies, and within our solar system the degree of order is breath-taking. The ancients looked for the rising of the star Sirius over the Nile at dawn, knowing that this would be repeated 365 days, 6 hours, 9 minutes and 9.6 seconds later—a sidereal year. Such is the order in the solar system that we can send space-probes on predetermined paths. Everywhere in the universe we see order and available energy. This is not what we would expect to see as the outcome of an explosion (Rosevear, *Creation Science*, p. 33).

Duane Gish writes about the probability of an original big bang:

This huge cosmic egg then exploded—and here we are today, several billion years later, human beings with a three-pound brain composed of twelve billion neurons each connected to about ten thousand other neurons in the most complicated arrangement of matter known to man. (There are thus 120 trillion connections in the human brain).

If this is true, then what we are and how we came to be were due solely to the properties inherent in electrons, protons, and neutrons. To believe this obviously requires a tremendous exercise of faith (Duane T. Gish, *Evolution: The Challenge of the Fossil Record*, San Diego: Creation-Life Publishers, 1985, pp. 24,25).

Not Scriptural

Apart from the scientific problems connected with the big bang theory, it cannot be reconciled with what the Bible teaches concerning origins. What is presented in Genesis 1:1 has no relationship to the modern-day big bang theory. According to Scripture, the earth did not begin as an incandescent fireball but was created in the beginning with a surface covered with water. The earth did *not* come about as a result of some explosion.

Series Of Commands

In addition, the Bible says God created the universe, light and life itself through a series of commands. The hypothetical big bang would have God doing very little work after the initial explosion. The non-involvement of God, as the big bang theory assumes, is at odds with Scripture because God was intimately involved in His creation. The big bang theory teaches a "hands off" universe as Lambert Dolphin explains:

> The Big Bang Model means a "hands off universe." The whole idea of the big bang is that the history of the universe is totally determined once the initial conditions have been fixed. No real room for subsequent intervention by God . . . Any divine intervention would upset the delicate balance rendering the present cosmology incorrect. This contrasts with a universe formed and fashioned in every detail by a loving Craftsman . . . The non-involvement of God . . . is presupposed by this theory. This cannot be established from Scripture as the way things really happened. "Let there be light" is a powerful command of God, calling light into existence. For the Son of God merely to roll back the cloud layer covering the earth so as to let light from space to shine on the earth would be a trivial command. Likewise for most of the creative work of God to be condensed into the "the creation event", i.e. the hypothetical big bang explosion, leaves God very little work to do during the ensuing six days. The Christian church has always understood God as having spoken the universe into existence by a series of commands. This is brought out in John chapter one. If most of the important work of creating the universe is over and done with by the end of Genesis 1:2, the commands that follow on the remaining five days are miniscule in comparison, except for the emergence of life. However the commands that bring life into being are weighed equally with the rest of the spoken words of God calling everything into being (Lambert Dolphin, Critique of Hugh Ross, n.d., p. 5).

In addition, the Bible seems to indicate that creation was instantaneous:

By the word of the Lord the heavens were made, and all the host of them by the breath of His mouth . . . For He spoke and it was done; He commanded, and it stood fast (Psalm 33:6,9).

Scientist Donald Chittick comments:

Some Christians wondered whether the big bang might be the creation event described in Genesis. However, it is wrong to confuse the postulated big bang with creation. It is a philosophical mistake because the big bang explanation was invented as a philosophical alternative to creation. It did not come from a study of Scripture. The big bang is a mechanistic or naturalistic explanation. It is an antisupernatural explanation of origins (Donald Chittick, *The Controversy*, Portland: Multnomah Press, 1984, p. 62).

Summary

The big bang theory attempts to explain the origin of the universe in a non-supernatural way. Though some Christians attempt to equate the big bang with the creation of Genesis 1:1, it is not an advisable thing to do. David E. O'Brien perceptively writes:

In the past hundred years many have tried to establish linkages between the spare, beautiful account of Genesis 1 and the emerging details of what are still infant sciences. The best of these disturb me, for one simple reason. It's been tried before and the results have always been disastrous
. . . .
It's a monumental blunder when we support a questionable biblical interpretation with questionable science, but an even more incredible blunder when we adopt a scientific world view as "biblical" and then use Scripture to support it (David E. O'Brien, *Today's Handbook for Solving Bible Difficulties*, Minneapolis: Bethany House Publishers, 1990, p. 169).

9

DOES THE BIBLE GIVE
AN AGE TO THE EARTH?

One of the most important questions in the Bible/science controversy concerns the age of the earth. How old is it? Does the Bible give a precise age to the earth? If the earth and universe are billions of years old can this be reconciled with the Bible?

Evolution

Today the earth is assumed to be approximately 4.6 billion years old while the universe is believed to be at least 10 to 15 billions years of age. For the theory of evolution to be true, it is necessary that the earth be very old. For life to spontaneously develop from an original single cell to our present complex universe, billions of years are needed.

Scientist E. H. Andrews, who believes the earth is young, lists the basic arguments of those who believe it is old:

The argument for an ancient earth (aged approximately 4.5 thousand million years according to our current estimate) fall into three main categories. First, come the arguments from cosmogony, involving the length of time required for the earth to form from interstellar matter . . . The second category of evidence concerns the rates of formation of sedimentary rocks and other geological processes such as mountain building and continental drift. The third type of evidence is that of radiometric dating (E. H. Andrews, *Creation and Evolution*, Derek Burke editor, Oxford: University Press, 1985, p. 49).

To many, arguments such as these confirm the theory that the earth is old.

What Do Christians Believe?

Many people have misconceptions regarding what Christians believe about the age of the earth. The following is a typical example:

The fundamentalist argument against the scientific assertion of the great age of our planet—to the effect that God created the earth only about 6,000 years ago, including fossils embedded in rocks—is unworthy of serious discussion. If we begin with the assumption that God can do anything he pleases, then of course he could have made the world 6,000 years ago, or last Tuesday, and planted *misleading evidence suggesting it was billions of years older* (italics his) (Steve Allen, *Steve Allen on Religion, The Bible, and Morality*, Buffalo: Prometheus Books, 1990, p. 19).

This argument is hardly worthy of serious discussion. First, the Bible does not put a date on the creation of the universe. Second, the Bible does not say, and no serious Christian teaches, that God created the earth with fossils embedded in the rocks to fool unbelieving scientists.

No Precise Age

There are many Christians, both scientists and theologians, who accept the idea of an old universe. Geologist William Tanner writes:

The rock record, despite diligent search by many determined to find positive evidence of a brief earth history has not revealed any such evidence . . . . Geology *requires* a very long history, and the Bible *permits* a very long history . . . The simplest best statement of fact concerning the creation controversy is: we do not yet know the final word, but the evidence points strongly in the direction of a torturously slow development, as God's purposes have been carried out according to the schedule of His choosing (W. F. Tanner, "Time and the Rock Record," *Journal of American Scientific Affiliation*, 33, 1981, pp. 100-105)

Christians who believe the earth is old usually view the "days" recorded in Genesis as referring to long periods of time. Others argue that the entire creation account is only supposed to be understood figuratively. This allows modern science, rather than Scripture, to give us information concerning the age of the earth and universe.

4004 B.C.?

A popular view is that the earth was created about six thousand years ago in 4004 B.C. This date of creation is usually associated with the work of Archbishop James Ussher (1581-1656), although others in Ussher's day arrived at the same figure. Ussher, working with the genealogical tables in the Book of Genesis and assuming them to be complete, deduced there were 4004 years from the creation of the world to the birth of Christ. Ussher's chronology eventually made its way into the margin of various English translations of the Bible. Ian Taylor explains:

In 1701 the date 4004 B.C. for the year of creation was inserted as a marginal commentary in the English edition of the Great Bible by Bishop Lloyd and, by association, thus being incorporated into the dogma of the Christian church. By the time the theory of evolution came into open conflict with church dogma, almost every Bible published in the nineteenth century had Ussher's date appended to the first page, followed by the sequential dates throughout to the time of the birth of Christ. As the church succumbed to the reasonings of science, these dates were quietly dropped from the Bible's beginning around the turn of this century (Ian Taylor, *In the Minds of Men*, Revised Edition, Toronto: TFE Publishing, 1987, p. 284).

Many have ridiculed the early dating of the creation of the world, such as the atheist Robert Ingersoll:

And first, let us examine the account given of the Creation of this world, commenced, according to the bible, on Monday morning about five thousand eight hundred and eighty-three years ago. The problem is compounded by the chronology given by Archbishop Ussher and still printed in some editions of the King James Bible (Robert Ingersoll, *Some Mistakes of Moses*, p. 55).

Date Unknown

We do not know exactly when the earth was created because the Bible does not tell us. Though this idea, that the Bible teaches Adam was created in 4004 B.C., is still brought up by some, it is not what the Bible teaches. Even those who advocate the recent creation view do not accept Ussher's chronology as the exact date of creation.

The 4004 B.C. date of creation is inaccurate because the genealogies in Genesis that Ussher used to calculate the years from the creation to Christ are incomplete. It is not a simple thing to add up the various years listed from the time of Adam. The late Bible scholar Merrill Unger wrote:

It is highly improbable that the genealogical framework of Gen 5 was intended to be used or can be used, for calculating the number of years (1656) between the creation of man and the Flood, thus dating man's creation 4004 B.C., (Ussher). There are several reasons: (1) The Hebrew terms 'begat,' 'son,' 'daughter' are used with great latitude and may involve a distant as well as immediate descendant. (2) The ten generations from Adam to Noah and the ten from Noah to Abraham evidently aim at brevity and symmetry, rather than an unbroken father-to-son relation. (3) Abbreviations due to symmetry are common features of Scripture genealogies (as in Mt 1). (4) In the recurring formula A lived—years and begat B, and A lived after he begat B—years and begat sons and daughters, B may not be the literal son of A. If so, the age of A may be his age when his descendant was born from whom B was descended. An indefinite time interval may therefore be intended between A and B (Merrill Unger, *The New Unger's Bible Handbook*, revised by Gary L. Larsen, Chicago: Moody Press, 1984, pp. 36,37).

Not Unlimited Time

Though we cannot date the earth with exact precision because of gaps in the genealogies we should not assume that the gaps provide us with an unlimited amount of time to date the earth. Theologian John Whitcomb writes:

In the first place, to stretch the genealogies of Genesis 5 and 11 to cover a period of over a hundred thousand years is to do violence to the chronological framework of all subsequent biblical history. By means of biblical analogies, it is indeed possible to find gaps, especially in the genealogies of Genesis 11. But those very analogies serve to limit our time scale for Genesis 11. The gap between Amram and Moses was three hundred years, not thirty thousand (cf. Exod. 6:20; Num 3:17-19, 27-28). And the gap between Joram and Uzziah in Matthew 1:8 was fifty years, not five thousand.

In the second place, only three of the ten patriarchs listed in Genesis 11—Rue, Serug, and Nahor—are available for spanning the vast period of time demanded by these anthropologists, for the patriarchs listed before them preceded the Tower of Babel judgment and the scattering of mankind (cf. Gen. 10:25). And yet the clearest suggestion of a time gap in Genesis 11 occurs before this judgment between Eber and Peleg, because of the sudden drop in life span.

In the third place, it is impossible to imagine that Reu, Serug, and Nahor, to say nothing of Lamech, Noah and Shem, were savage illiterate cave dwellers of the stone-age period. The fourth chapter of Genesis, with its clear indication of cultural achievement, including the forging of "all implements of bronze and iron" (vs. 22), and Genesis 6, with its account of the great ark-building project, make such a theory completely untenable. Or are we to suppose that in some tiny pocket of civilization, nearly swamped by an ocean of human savagery, an unbroken chain of saintly men (some who lived for centuries) perpetuated the Messianic line of Shem and handed down the knowledge of the one true God for hundreds of thousands of years? Even to ask such a question is to answer it (John Whitcomb, *The Early Earth*, Revised edition, Grand Rapids: Baker Book House, 1986, p. 133).

Theoretically, creationists are able to work with an old earth or a young earth. Though Scripture gives us no clear evidence as to the precise age of the earth, it suggests that man has appeared on the scene rather recently. The idea of an earth that is billion years old is nowhere taught in Scripture. Old Testament authority Oswald Allis wrote:

We need to remember that limitless time is a poor substitute for that Omnipotence which can dispense with time. The reason the account of creation given here is so simple and so impressive is that it speaks in terms of the creative acts of an omnipotent God, and not in terms of *limitless* space and *infinite* time and *endless* process (Oswald T. Allis, *God Spake By Moses*, Grand Rapids: Baker Book House, 1951, p. 11, (emphasis his).

How Old Is The Earth?

What do we know for certain? Contrary to popular belief, there is no certain or unequivocal evidence that the earth is older than a few thousand years. Written records only take us back a few thousand years. Anthropologist and archaeologist Colin Renfrew writes:

The Egyptian king lists go back to the First Dynasty of Egypt, a little before 3000 B. C. Before that, there were no written records anywhere (Colin Renfrew, *Before Civilization*, New York: Alfred Knopf, 1973, p. 25).

What happened before this time is based on conjecture. Henry Morris writes:

Prior to written history, of course, chronologists are forced to rely on various changing physical systems (e.g. decaying radioactive minerals, eroding continents, buildup of chemicals in oceans) for time estimates. Such calculations must always be based on the various assumptions of uniformitarianism (e.g. system isolated, rate of change constant, initial composition known), none of which assumptions are provable, testable or even reasonable. The radiocarbon method, for example, is now known to be so unreliable that many archaeologists have abandoned it altogether (Henry Morris with Gary Parker, *What is Creation Science?*, Revised edition, El Cajon, Calif.: Master Books, 1987, p. 14).

Different Quality Of Time

Some scientists believe that there was a different quality to time before the fall. Lambert Dolphin writes:

I personally think time as we know it now began with the fall of man and that time had different qualities before the fall . . . . .

The fact that the creative activity of God took place in a time sequence from Day One through Day Seven indicates that time was "flowing" in its usual sense through the present towards the future. Yet . . . there is an eternal dimension also present all through creation week. Neither Satan nor Adam had fallen, there was yet no sin. "Perfect physics" prevailed, and the spiritual dimension of the universe was "in tune" with the physical in a way we cannot now exactly understand (Lambert Dolphin, *Jesus: Lord of Space and Time*, Green Forest, Arizona: New Leaf Press, 1988, p. 70).

Unable To Find Out

The Bible hints that we may not be able to resolve this issue:

He has made everything beautiful in its time. Also he has put eternity in their hearts, except that *no one can find out* the work that God does from the beginning (Ecclesiastes 3:11, emphasis added).

This passage may indicate that the issue of the age of the earth may be beyond our finding out.

Summary

The theory of evolution demands that the earth and universe be old while special creation can have either a young or old earth. Though the Bible does not us give an *exact* age of the earth, there is no indication in Scripture that the earth is very old. The genealogies in Scripture do not allow an unlimited amount of time between Adam and Abraham.

Scientific evidence has been brought forward that would indicate the earth may be young after all but there is no consensus among Christians. Most scientists, Christian and non-Christian, believe the earth and universe are old. The age of the earth is not an issue that has been settled among believers. Scientist Paul Zimmerman writes:

Thus the evolutionist needs a very old earth. His theory is utterly hopeless if the earth is young . . . On the other hand the creationist can operate with a young earth or a very ancient one . . . The creationist does not need millions of years to make his theory workable. For the believer in creation the question is a different one: (1) What does the Bible say about the date of creation? (2) Is this information at variance with the facts brought to light by scientific research? These questions the creationist seeks to answer . . . Actually neither the scientist nor the creationist can fix the date of the beginning. The Bible permits certain general conclusions, but it does not give the age of the earth. The scientist in turn can make certain interesting calculations, but his computations are often interlarded with slippery assumptions, and the results are beclouded by serious questions that rise in the research (P. A. Zimmerman, "The Age of the Earth," in *Darwin*,

Evolution and Creation, P.A. Zimmerman, ed; St. Louis: Concordia, 1959, pp. 144,145).

It is also possible that time had a different quality before sin entered the universe. This would make it impossible for us to pinpoint the time of creation.

Concerning the age of the earth, Mark Twain wryly commented:

> In the space of one hundred and seventy-six years the lower Mississippi has shortened itself two hundred and forty-two miles. This is an average of a trifle over one mile and a third per year. Therefore, any calm person, who is not blind or idiotic, can see that in the Old Oolitic Silurian period just a million years ago next November, the lower Mississippi river was upward of one million three hundred thousand miles long and stuck out over the Gulf of Mexico like a fishing rod. And, by the same token, any person can see that seven hundred and forty-two years from now, the lower Mississippi will be only a mile and three-quarters long, and Cairo and New Orleans will have joined their streets together, and be plodding comfortably along with a single mayor and a mutual board of Alderman. There is something fascinating about science. One gets such wholesale returns out of such a trifle investment of fact (Samuel L. Clemens, *Life on the Mississippi*, New York: Harper and Brothers, 1874, p. 156).

We again want to emphasize that the age of the earth is not the main issue in the Bible/science debate; it is chance versus design. Old Testament authority Ronald Youngblood offers a fitting conclusion:

> No one knows for certain, of course, when the beginning was. But the Old Testament is far more interested in the fact of creation than the time of creation, and the simple truth that God's creative activity took place during an indeterminate time known as "the beginning" was joyfully celebrated by poet (Ps. 102.25) and prophet (Isa. 40:21) alike (Ronald Youngblood, *How It All Began*, Ventura, California: Regal Books, 1980, p. 22).

10

WHAT IS THE EVOLUTIONARY VIEW OF THE ORIGIN OF LIFE?

The theory of evolution teaches that life originated by chance, not by design. How and why it happened is unknown. Science writer Isaac Asimov has admitted that any explanation is guesswork:

We can make inspired guesses, but we don't know for certain what physical and chemical properties of the planet's crust, its ocean and its atmosphere made it so conducive to such a sudden appearance of life. We are not certain about the amount and forms of energy that permeated the environment in the planet's early days. Thus the problem that scientists face is how to explain the suddenness in which life appeared on this young (4.6 billion year old) planet earth. In the nineteenth century, scientists first began to accept the concept of biological evolution and to dismiss the possibility that life had been created in its present complexity by some supernatural agency. That raised the question of how this extraordinary phenomenon called life could possibly have come to be by accident (Isaac Asimov, *Omni*, November 1983, p. 58).

Life Arose By Chance

The theory of evolution maintains that when the earth was formed a few billion years ago it had an atmosphere (called a reducing atmosphere) that was radically different from today. It is assumed that no oxygen was present in the early earth's atmosphere. The atmosphere supposedly consisted of methane, ammonia, hydrogen, and water vapor. If the early earth had oxygen in its atmosphere as it has today, life could not have spontaneously evolved. Oxygen breaks down big molecules into smaller ones, and would have destroyed the large molecules long before they reached the state of living.

It is believed that life originally emerged through a fortunate situation in some primeval pool of water. Molecules were randomly and spontaneously formed by the action of ultraviolet rays, electrical discharges, and a continuous bombardment of highly charged particles. More and more pieces clustered together and formed increasingly larger molecules and molecular chains. Through random processes these giant molecules then combined until a primitive cell stage was reached. Finally, they absorbed other molecules and, at some point, began to produce. Thus developed the first living cells. Those first living cells then fed on the molecules still left in the "primeval soup."

Soon thereafter photosynthetic cells developed which produced and released oxygen into the atmosphere. That oxygen, combined with the metabolism of those first living cells, destroyed the original molecules and changed the atmosphere forever. Once life had evolved, the theory of evolution teaches that the earth's environment was so altered that life could no longer develop spontaneously.

Laws Of Probability

What are the chances that life could develop spontaneously in the hypothetical primeval soup by chance and over long periods of time? They are not very good. One single bacterium, for example, contains some 1,500 enzymes, which, in turn, consist of several hundred amino acids. Those various amino acids must be arranged in precisely the right sequence. The chance that a given enzyme, consisting of two hundred amino acids (of which there are twenty different kinds) could develop by chance is one in 20^{200}. In other words, the chance is practically non-existent. And that is only one of the necessary 1,500 enzymes for one bacterium. The origin of a single living cell, then, would require billions of kilos of each of the many different enzymes and DNA molecules, combining and recombining randomly, until, against all probability, just the right random combination occurred.

Furthermore, there is now overwhelming evidence that the earth's early atmosphere was not a reducing atmosphere. It may have had more oxygen than today!

Not Enough Time

It is often said by evolutionists that given enough time life could spontaneously develop. Nobel prize winning scientist George Wald has stated:

> The important point is that since the origin of life belongs to the category of 'at-least-once' phenomena, time is on its side. However improbable we regard this event, or any of the steps it involves, given enough time, it will almost certainly happen at least once. And for life as we know it, with its capability for growth and reproduction, once may be enough. Time is the hero of the plot . . . Given so much time, the impossible becomes possible, the possible becomes probable, the probable becomes virtually certain. One only has to wait; time itself performs miracles (George Wald, "The Origin of Life," *Scientific American*, August, 1954, p. 45).

There is the famous statement of Julian Huxley that given enough time monkeys typing on typewriters could eventually type out the complete works of Shakespeare. The idea that time can solve all the problems is just not true. Luther Sunderland writes:

> Such uninformed statements have a dramatic effect on the layman, and even persons who have the mathematical background to know better would reveal the ridiculousness of the conjecture. For example, if there were monkeys typing

on typewriters covering every square foot of the Earth's surface and each one typed at the random fantastic rate of ten characters a second for 30 billion years, there would not be the slightest reasonable chance that a single one would type out a single specific five word sentence of 31 letters, spaces, and punctuation. (The actually probability is less than one chance in a trillion). Yet Huxley was permitted to make such a preposterous statement that monkeys could type out the complete works of Shakespeare, and no evolutionary scientist or mathematician who knew better raised a single objection.

Time definitely is not the hero of the plot. In reality, time destroys the assumptions of evolutionary theory—even the 20 billion years assumed by the big bang. If a single five-word sentence could not be formed in more time than the earth has existed, it is even less conceivable that the data contained in the genes of a single cell could have formed by random processes, because the genes of the simplest single-celled organism contain more data that there are letters in all of the volumes of the world's largest library (Luther Sunderland, *Darwin's Enigma: Fossils and Other Problems*, 4th Edition, Revised and expanded, El Cajon, Calif.: Master Book Publishers, 1988, pp. 61,62).

Hard To Believe

The difficulty of believing the evolutionary scenario is further described by scientist Henry Morris:

The marvel of life on earth only can be explained by creation. One of the strangest phenomena of our supposedly scientific age is the insistent faith held by many scientists that somewhere, somehow life has arisen from non-life by naturalistic evolutionary processes. Science is supposed to be based on facts and knowledge, not speculation and wishful thinking. The law of biogenesis, based on all the observed data and biology and chemistry, states that life comes only from life. The doctrine from abiogenesis, on the other hand, teaches that certain unknown conditions in the primitive atmosphere and ocean acted upon certain mysterious chemicals existing at that time to synthesize still more complex chemicals, whatever they were, constituted the original living systems from which all living organisms later evolved.

Thus primitive unknown life forms which no longer exist were derived from unknown chemicals by unknown processes which no longer operate, in an atmosphere of exotic and unknown composition in contact with the primitive oceanic soup of unknown structure! This remarkable construct is today taught as sober science in our public schools, in spite of the fact that there is not one single scientific observation to demonstrate that such things ever happened or even could happen (Henry Morris, *The Remarkable Birth of Planet Earth*, Minneapolis: Bethany Fellowship, Inc., 1972, pp. 34,35).

Astronomer Sir Fred Hoyle, the inventor of the Steady State Theory of the origin of the universe, was an atheist most of his life. In his later years he changed his mind because of the impossibility of life developing by chance. He said the probability that life could have developed by chance is the same as, "a tornado sweeping through a junkyard would assemble a Boeing 747 from the materials therein" (Sir Fred Hoyle, "Hoyle on Evolution," *Nature*, Vol. 294, Nov. 12, 1981, p. 105).

Hoyle also wrote:

The likelihood of the formation of life from inanimate matter is one to a number with 40,000 noughts after it . . . It is big enough to bury Darwin and the whole theory of evolution. There was no primeval soup, neither on this planet nor on any other, and if the beginnings of life were not random, they must therefore have been the product of purposeful intelligence (Sir Fred Hoyle, "Hoyle on Evolution," p. 105).

Hoyle's colleague Chandra Wickramasinghe concluded:

From my earliest training as a scientist, I was very strongly brainwashed to believe science cannot be consistent with any kind of deliberate creation. That notion has been painfully shed. At the moment I can't find any rational argument to knock down the view that argues for conversion to God . . . Now we realize the only logical answer to life is creation (interview in the *London Daily Express*, August 14, 1981).

Life Brought To Earth?

Because of the great odds of life forming spontaneously there are some scientists who have suggested that life was somehow brought to earth from another planet. This is known as directed panspermia. Francis Crick, who shared the Nobel prize for the discovery of DNA's structure, is now convinced that life could not and did not evolve on earth. In his book, *Life Itself,* he argues for "directed panspermia." Crick realizes that his view only moves the question of origins back to another time and place but he feels he is compelled to make such a suggestion because of the odds of life developing by chance here on the earth. He wrote:

What is so frustrating to our present purpose is that it seems almost impossible to give any numerical value for the probability of what seems a rather unlikely sequence of events . . . An honest man, armed with all the knowledge available to us now, could only state that in some sense, the origin of life appears at the moment to be almost a miracle . . . But if it turns out that it was rather unlikely, then we are compelled to consider whether it might have arisen in other places in the Universe where possibly, for one reason or another, conditions were more favorable (Francis Crick, *Life Itself*, New York: Simon and Schuster, 1981, pp. 87,88).

E.T.?

Leading evolutionist William D. Hamilton of Oxford University theorizes that mankind might be the "experiment" of some alien intelligence.

There's one theory of the universe that I rather like . . . Suppose our planet is a "zoo for extraterrestrial beings"; they planted the seeds of evolution on earth hoping to create interesting intelligent creatures. "And they watched their experiments, interfering hardly at all. So that almost everything we do comes out according to the laws of nature. But every now and then they see something which doesn't look quite right." For example: "This zoo is going to kill itself off if they let you do this or that. So they insert a finger and just change some little thing. And maybe those are the miracles which the religious people like to so emphasize" (cited by Robert Wright, "Science, God and Man," *Time*, December 28, 1992, p. 44).

This theory reduces humans to being pets of some alien zookeeper. If the God of the Bible is left out of the picture, this type of speculation is the logical result.

Too Young And Too Small

Even if one accepts the universe is 13 billions years old, it is still too young and too small for life to have life developed by chance.

Since the universe is simply too young and too small to account for its appearance (even at 13 billion years and 30 billion light-years across), we are forced to asked, "From where did it come?" The logical answer is that it came from a supreme Intelligence! Not only is this logical, it is the simplest answer (Robert Gange, *Origins and Destiny*, Dallas, Word Publishing: 1986, p. 71).

Summary

The evolutionary idea of life spontaneously appearing is not supported by the facts. Even billions of years will not allow this to happen. This has led some non-Christian scientists to argue for life being brought to earth from some other planet. This shows the lack of a scientific basis that life came into existence by chance. The best answer is that it was created by an Intelligent Being who has lovingly designed this universe for His special creation—man.

11

CAN LIFE COME
FROM NON-LIFE?

A few centuries ago, most people believed that life developed spontaneously. This is known as the theory of spontaneous generation. It was believed, for example, that flies could develop from rotting meat. It took two centuries for the scientific opponents of this idea to convince everyone that life can only come from life. Numerous experiments showed that if the proper sanitary precautions were taken, such as preventing flies from laying eggs in the meat, no new life developed.

Louis Pasteur

It was the experiments of Louis Pasteur that settled the matter. Pasteur took broth, thoroughly boiled it, and then sealed it off to prevent contamination of new microbes. The broth stayed completely clear and sterile. There was no new life.

Those who still believed in spontaneous generation claimed that the proper nourishment from the air could not reach the broth, and that was why life did not develop in Pasteur's mixture. Pasteur then constructed a glass container that allowed air to circulate over the broth, but prevented microbes from reaching it. Again, the broth remained clear and sterile.

He had proven his hypothesis. The universally accepted scientific law became that life cannot develop from nonliving matter.

It is a curious fact that the same scientists who believe that life cannot now come from non-life also believe that life did develop from non-life several billion years ago. What is impossible to happen today was possible in the past. These scientists realize the inconsistency of their position, but they believe that past conditions then were radically different than they are today. The problem with holding this view is that no evidence exists that conditions in the early earth were radically different from today's conditions. It is merely an assumption that is not supported by any evidence. Yet most scientists and most introductory science texts present the existence of such a primeval soup and primeval atmosphere as an established fact.

Illogical Thinking

This type of reasoning is not logical. The fact that life now exists does not prove things had to have been radically different at the beginning and that life came from nonlife. This entire theory contains only one fact: life exists today. Nothing has been demonstrated to show either:

(1)   that life came from nonlife, or

(2)   that things were "radically different" enough for life to have been able to come from nonlife.

Harvard scientist George Wald wrote:

Many scientists a century ago chose to regard the belief in spontaneous generation as a philosophical necessity. It is a symptom of the philosophical poverty of our time that this necessity is no longer appreciated. Most modern biologists, having reviewed with satisfaction the downfall of the spontaneous generation hypothesis, yet unwilling to accept the alternative belief in special creation, are left with nothing (George Wald, "The Origin of Life," *Scientific American*, August 1954, p. 46).

Life In A Test Tube?

All attempts to simulate the conditions of the early earth and create life in a test tube have failed. Most modern textbooks on biology point to the experiments of Stanley Miller in the 1950's as to how life originally formed in the primeval soup. Miller attempted to create life from non-life in a laboratory setting by duplicating the supposed atmosphere of the early earth. Out of his experiments certain molecules were produced that are important building blocks of life. Miller accomplished this by subjecting the atmosphere to electrical charges and then immediately trapping the molecules that were formed as a result of the reaction. He had to trap the molecules since those same electrical charges that formed them would disintegrate them with their next charges. Yet nature contains no such "trap." If these molecules were randomly produced by nature they would have been immediately destroyed.

Unstable Molecules

In addition, Miller's experiments also produced biologically unusable molecules. In actuality Miller's experiments complicated the problem for evolutionists. Did the so-called primeval atmosphere have both kinds of molecules? If this is true, then how did the life-building molecules disassociate themselves from other molecules long enough to combine and form the first living cell? If the atmosphere of the early earth were not the same as in Miller's experiments, then what was it and why did it only produce life giving molecules? Miller's experiments, far from proving how life originally arose on earth, raises more questions than answers. It must be emphasized that Miller never produced one living cell in his experiments. Phillip E. Johnson writes:

> Geochemists now report that the atmosphere of the early earth was not of the strongly reducing nature required for the Miller-Urey apparatus to give the desired results. Even under ideal and probably unrealistic conditions, the experiments failed to produce some of the necessary chemical components of life. Perhaps the most discouraging

criticism came from chemists, who have spoiled the prebiotic soup by showing that organic compounds produced on the early earth would be subject to chemical reactions making them unsuitable for constructing life. In all probability, the prebiotic soup could never have existed, and without it there is no reason to believe that the production of small amounts of some amino acids by electrical charge in a reducing atmosphere had anything to do with the origin of life (Phillip E. Johnson, *Darwin on Trial*, Downers Grove, Illinois: InterVarsity Press, 1991, p. 103).

Produced By Intelligence

If someday we do create life in a test tube it will not have been done by chance, but by a designer, an intelligent being. However, it will not tell us *how* life actually did originate. Any type of simulated experiment would only be one explanation among several on how life actually developed. Phillip E. Johnson notes:

Although these objections to the Miller-Urey results are important, for present purposes I prefer to disregard them as a distraction from the main point. Let us grant that, one way or another, all required chemical components were present on the early earth. That still leaves us at a dead end, because there is no reason to believe that life has a tendency to emerge when the right chemicals are sloshing about in a soup. Although some components of living systems can be duplicated with very advanced technology, scientists employing the full power of their intelligence cannot manufacture living organisms from amino acids, sugars, and the like. How then was the trick done before scientific intelligence was in existence? (Phillip E. Johnson, *Darwin on Trial*, p. 103).

Theologian Bernard Ramm writes:

At our present state of knowledge two things may be stated. (i) Man has not produced life chemically. That he may produce protoplasmic specks . . . is a possibility, but the production of even the smallest organism is as yet a long time away. In view of our inability to produce life with our vast chemical knowledge and our ability to reproduce almost any condition we wish . . . we must still view a chance origin of life as a faith and not as a verified hypothesis. (ii) Unless a person is very anti-Christian it cannot be denied that the most satisfactory explanation to date is that life is the creation of the Living God. There is certainly nothing scientifically disrespectable in this connection, even though a person is not a believer. Those who do believe it, may do so without fear of contravening scientific fact and without prejudicing the character of their judgment . . . . Science is still unable to put forward any satisfactory explanation as to how life arose in the first place. We must either accept the Bible doctrine that God created life, or go on making improbable speculations (Bernard Ramm, *The Christian View Of Science And Scripture,* Grand Rapids: Eerdmans, 1954, p. 183).

Can It Be Done?

Award-winning scientist, E.H. Andrews, explains the chain of events that must have happened if life originally developed by chance:

> The early atmosphere had to contain some small molecules and not others.
> Lightning or ultra-violet light had to be present to make them link together, but not to break them down again.
> The new, larger molecules had to be washed down by rain. The molecules had to be below the clouds for this to happen, but the small ammonia molecules which dissolve very easily in water, were somehow not washed out of the sky. (This is hard to believe is it not?)
> The larger molecules, though not very soluble in water, had to stay in the water as it filtered through the soil and ran over the rocks.
> These molecules, though lighter than water, had to remain under the water. If they floated to the surface, they would have been destroyed by ultra-violet light.

The molecules had to collect and become concentrated in the organic soup so that they could be made to link together.

There had to be some very special catalyst molecules to make the inorganic molecules link up with water.

The right organic molecules had to be present in the right amounts to link up into proteins and DNA. Somehow, the special coded order of proteins and DNA had to happen. No convincing or even possible explanation for this has yet been given.

Organic droplets had to form and stay around long enough for something to happen inside them which would turn them into living cells. No one knows how something like this could happen.

Finally, of course, the first living cell had to find out how to divide before it died (single cell animals do not live very long lives, especially in strong solutions of ammonia which we use to kill germs today).

Here we have eleven steps, each of which had to be just right for life to survive. None of these steps separately is completely impossible, though we have no idea how one or two of them could have happened. But strung together to give an explanation of the origin of life they add up to a very unlikely story! (E. H. Andrews, *From Nothing to Nature*, Durham, England: Evangelical Press, 1978, pp. 41, 42).

It seems that some non-Christian scientists are beginning to admit the impossibility of life coming from non-life. *Time* magazine reports.

Presumably if you let simple molecules reshuffle themselves randomly for long enough, some complex ones would get formed, and further reshuffling would make them more complex, until you had something like DNA—a stable molecule that just happened to make copies of itself.

But more recent, more careful analysis suggests that even a mildly impressive living molecule is quite unlikely to form randomly. Then where did it come from? (Robert Wright, "Science, God, and Man," *Time*, December 28, 1992, p. 40).

Summary

Life does not come from non-life. This is a scientific fact. There is a big difference between a dead cell and a living one, or a dead body and a living person. If life ever were created in a test tube it would show intelligence is need to bring it about. Gary Parker writes:

> Chemistry, then is not our ancestor, it's our problem ... Time and chance are no help to the evolutionist either, since time and chance can only act on inherent chemical properties. Trying to throw 'life' on a roll of molecular dice is like trying to throw a '13' on a pair of gambling dice. It just won't work. The possibility is not there, so the probability is just plain zero (Gary Parker and Henry Morris, *What is Creation Science?*, Revised edition, El Cajon, Calif.: Master Books, p. 40).

The Bible says the earth did not start with a reducing atmosphere of hydrogen, methane, and ammonia which eventually developed into our present-day oxygen-rich atmosphere. Rather, it was created with sufficient oxygen to support plant and animal life. Furthermore, life did not evolve in water; it started on land when God created vegetation on the third day (Genesis 1:11,12). Life did not come from "non-life" but rather from the Giver of Life.

12

IS THE UNIVERSE DECAYING?

The theory of evolution teaches that the universe is developing from simple to higher levels of complexity. The Bible teaches that everything was created perfect but now is deteriorating because of the entrance of sin. Is the universe deteriorating or it is going onward to higher levels of complexity?

The laws of thermodynamics provide some of the strongest scientific arguments for the existence of a Creator. Though scientific "laws" are only theories that can be modified as the evidence dictates, the First and Second Laws of Thermodynamics, however, are the basis of all science. Simply stated, they are as follows:

First Law

The First Law of Thermodynamics is the Law of the conservation of energy. It teaches that although energy can be converted from one form to another, the total amount remains unchanged; that is, energy cannot be created or destroyed. Thus, there can be no new creation of material in the universe.

Second Law

The Second Law of Thermodynamics, also known as the Law of Entropy, teaches that although the total amount of energy remains unchanged, there always becomes a tendency for it to become less available. The second law states that if any system is left to itself it will go on to randomness or disorder. The effect of this on the universe is that there will come a time when it will eventually "run out" of energy. Hence, the universe is deteriorating.

Creation Complete

How does this fit the creation model? The Bible teaches that creation is now finished:

Thus the heavens and the earth, and all the host of them, were finished. And on the seventh day God ended His work which He had done, and He rested on the seventh day from all His work which He had done (Genesis 2:1).

The Bible also teaches that the universe is running down as a result of the fall of man:

Of old You laid the foundation of the earth, and the heavens are the work of Your hands. They will perish, but You will endure; yes, all of them will grow old like a garment; like a cloak You will change them, and they will be changed (Psalm 102:25,26).

Problem For Evolutionists

There are problems reconciling the evolutionary theory with the law of entropy. The development of the living cell would require that nonliving matter spontaneously organize itself "upward" to much higher degrees of order, complexity and purposefulness. The Second Law of Thermodynamics says this does not happen in the universe. Evolutionists are aware of this, yet they still believe in the spontaneous development of life. They attempt to reconcile the problem by saying that the second law does not apply to the earth. It is only applicable in a "closed system," i. e., a system that does not exchange or receive energy from outside itself. The earth, they maintain, is not a closed system, but an open system which constantly receives abundant amounts of energy from the sun.

Something Else Is Needed

That answer is totally inadequate. Energy in and of itself contributes nothing to organization or design. Simply adding energy from the sun will give no developmental input to the random processes evolutionists describe for the origin of life. A pile of bricks and wood never would spontaneously develop into a building, no matter how much energy it received from the sun or how much time you gave it. Matter and energy by themselves provide insufficient causes for the complexity, design, and development we see around us. Scientist Bolton Davidheiser writes:

> Another way of looking at the second law of thermodynamics is that there is a trend toward randomness in the universe. That is, the trend is toward forming less complex distribution of matter and energy from more complex ones. A non-living structure left to itself tends to deteriorate and disintegrate. It falls apart and the pieces become scattered. A tornado can destroy a building, spreading its contents in a haphazard manner, but it will not assemble materials to form a building. The tendency toward randomness in nature is the opposite of evolution, for according to the theory of evolution, more complex forms developed from less complex forms (Bolton Davidheiser, *Evolution And Christian Faith*, Nutley, NJ: Presbyterian and Reformed Publishing Company, 1969, p. 221).

Program Needed

What is lacking is a "program" to organize matter and energy into higher levels of complexity and purposefulness. In order for a system to become more complex, it must have complexity added to it. When Christians say God is the Creator, they are saying there is a Designer behind the design. Christians have an adequate source for the development and complexity of the universe, while evolutionists have no adequate source for the world they see around them.

Though evolutionists have attempted to reconcile the two by factoring in energy from the sun, their attempts have failed. Energy is inadequate to account for the order, complexity, purpose and design we see in the created world around us. To maintain God as the Creator, is both reasonable and consistent with the Second Law of Thermodynamics. Gary Parker writes about the importance of a program and design:

> Can aluminum fly? I'm sure that sounds like a trick question. By itself, of course, aluminum can't fly. Aluminum ore in rock just sits there. A volcano may throw it, but it doesn't fly. If you pour gasoline on it, does that make it fly? Pour a little rubber on it; that doesn't make it fly either. But suppose you take that aluminum, stretch it out in a nice long tube with wings, a tail, and a few other parts. Then it flies; we call it an airplane.
>
> Did you ever wonder what makes an airplane fly? Try a few thought experiments. Take the wings off and study them; they don't fly. Take the engines off, study them; they don't fly. Don't dwell on this the next time you're on an airplane, but an airplane is a collection of non-flying parts. Not a single part of it flies!
>
> What does it take to make an airplane fly? The answer is something every scientist can understand and appreciate, something every scientist can work with and use to frame hypotheses and conduct experiments. What does it take to make an airplane fly. *Creative design and organization* (emphasis his) (Gary Parker, with Henry Morris, *What is Creation Science?*, Revised edition, El Cajon, Calif.: Master Books, 1987, p. 42).

Looking For New Law

Because the Second Law of Thermodynamics refutes the idea of progressive evolutionary development, secular scientists are looking for some yet undiscovered "new law" that would explain how order naturally rises out of disorder, how nature naturally organizes itself.

Science writer Robert Wright observes:

> Various scientists are pondering the prospect that a basic physical law lies waiting to be discovered, a law defining the circumstances under which systems infused with energy become more complexly structured. The law would carve out local exceptions to the general tendency of things to become more chaotic and bland—higher in "entropy"—as dictated by the famously depressing second law of thermodynamics. Charles H. Bennett, of IBM's Thomas J. Watson Research Center, who has deeply shaped the modern understanding of the second law, suspects there is indeed a law that if known would make life's origin less baffling. Such a law, he has said, would play a role "formerly assigned to God" (Robert Wright, "Science, God and Man," *Time*, December 28, 1992, p. 42.)

These statements illustrate the problem for evolutionists. The universe does not organize itself. Rather than admitting there is an "Organizer," secular scientists are now looking for some "law" that demonstrates that the universe does indeed organize itself. They are still unwilling to admit that the scientific evidence logically leads one to believe in the existence of a Designer.

It is also interesting to note that the term "depressing" is used here to describe the Second Law of Thermodynamics. It is depressing for evolutionists because it clearly testifies of the need of an intelligent Creator.

A new scientific field of study known as "complexity" has arisen to address this problem. Another science writer had this to say:

> If the basic rules of chemistry are any guide, life should not exist. Scientists showed in the 1950's that shooting an electric spark through a soup of chemicals—thus simulating lightning strikes on the primordial planet earth—could produce simple organic compounds. But complex, self-reproducing chemicals like DNA? They shouldn't have arisen in a trillion years. At an even deeper level, the second law of thermodynamics dictates that the universe should inexorably move toward disorganization.

Cups of tea always cool off; they never spontaneously get hotter. Iron rusts, but rust never turns into iron.

Yet over the eons, a chaotic universe organized itself into stars galaxies and planets. And at least one planet, our own, is now bursting with bewildering varieties, filled with organisms that have arrayed themselves into ecosystems, communities and complex societies. How did this happen? That is the question posed by a brand-new field of science known as complexity (J. Madeleine Nash, "Life, the Universe, and Everything," *Time*, February 22, 1993, p. 62)

Notice the leap of faith taken here. Everything in the universe testifies that life could not develop by chance and that life does not organize itself. This is what the facts state. Yet the writer goes on to say our universe did organize itself and life developed by blind chance. The statement is not made because of the evidence but because the writer has already *assumed* this is what must have happened. The conclusion is not based upon science nor scientific evidence. It is a philosophical statement based upon the writer's view of the world. It is typical of so many of the statements made by evolutionists.

What About Disorder?

Evolutionists often point to disorder or some small degree of imperfection in the universe to refute the idea of a Creator.

If order in the universe implies a Creator, does disorder imply a "non-Creator?" Did "chance" create some things while God created others?

The answer is no. When the vast reaches of the universe display such sophisticated intelligent design as we can observe today, the smaller degree of disorder serves as testimony to corruption of the grand design of the universe. That corruption is exactly what the Bible declares. God the Creator, of the universe, gave mankind the highest honor possible in the created order. The Bible describes the Lord's glory and the dignity which He gave mankind:

When I consider Your heavens, the work of your fingers, the moon and the stars, which You have ordained, What is man that You are mindful of him, and the Son of man that You visit him? For You have made him a little lower than the angels, and You have crowned him with glory and honor. You have made him to have dominion over the works of Your hands (Psalm 8:3-6).

God created man originally with dignity and authority. Mankind was the crown of God's creation.

Fall Of Man

When mankind deliberately broke his relationship with God, the entire creation felt, and continues to feel, the effects of that corruption. The Bible says that from the time that Adam and Eve sinned and were banished from God's presence, the effects of corruption have manifested themselves throughout the creation. The Apostle Paul, in his letter to the Romans, said:

For the earnest expectation of the creation eagerly waits for the revealing of the sons of God. For the creation was subject to futility, not willingly, but because of Him who subjected it in hope; because creation itself also will be delivered from the bondage of corruption into the glorious liberty of the children of God. For we know that the whole creation groans and labors with birth pangs together until now (Romans 8:19-22).

Summary

The Second Law of Thermodynamics testifies that everything in the universe is "winding down." This agrees with the creation model which says that everything was created perfect and then sin marred its perfection. Creationism teaches that every process in the universe is going from order to disorder. Evolutionists, having no answer to this scientific truth, are vainly searching for some "undiscovered law of science" that would show how lifeless objects organize themselves to higher degrees of complexity.

Furthermore, the presence of corruption in the universe does not contradict the testimony of the overall design and order in the universe to the existence of an intelligent and all-powerful Creator. It gives further testimony to the Fall of man.

Summary To Section Two

As we have examined the evidence for the origin of life and of the universe we find there is sufficient evidence for God as Creator. Our study has made it clear that life as we know it could not have evolved spontaneously or by chance. Evolution is incapable of giving an answer for the complexity of design we find everywhere evident in living organisms. Merely adding time to the equation will not solve the problem. Matter, energy, and time cannot accomplish complexity on their own. What is needed is a designer or programmer. Christians know that Designer as the Lord God.

Ultimately, any explanation as to what happened in the beginning must be done by faith. Ian Taylor writes:

> Naturalistic explanations are offered to explain away the miraculous but . . . they are often not really explanations at all. For example, a moment's thought given to the popular big-bang theory for the origin of the universe will show that it fails to account for the supposed highly-ordered primordial egg in the first place. Indeed, in the matter of origins, faith in the explanation offered is essential since there were no eye-witnesses to what actually happened nor can the event be repeated in a laboratory (Ian Taylor, *In the Minds of Men*, Revised edition, Toronto: TFE Publishing, 1987, p. 4).

The issue concerning origins comes down to believing in the God of the Bible or the god of chance. David E. O'Brien makes a fitting observation:

> I've been reading books on the debate between secularist science and biblical views of creation for almost thirty years, and the ease which the secularist scientists accept chance as a personal conscious being always astonishes me. The evidence of the created universe declares so powerfully that it was put here by an intelligence greater than man

that when God is refused His rightful place in the equation, chance usually becomes the deity who takes His place. "Chance decided," "chance decreed," "chance planned," are conclusions made by people who reject God as the source of everything.

No matter how distinguished scientists are, how many their degrees, or how impressive their publications, they can look pretty silly when, brought face-to-face with the inescapable reality of God, they have to explain that it wasn't really God (David E. O'Brien, *Today's Handbook for Solving Bible Difficulties*, Minneapolis: Bethany House Publishers, 1990, p. 165).

The important thing to note is that we *do* have a firsthand report of the creation of the universe. It is given to us by God. He was there at the beginning. He has given us His testimony in the Bible.

In our next section we will consider the controversial issue of creation and evolution.

Creation
And Evolution

Jesus said: "Have you not read that He who made them at the beginning made them male and female."
(Matthew 19:4)

13

WHAT IS THE THEORY OF EVOLUTION?

For the past one hundred years, the general theory of evolution has held the day in the scientific community, as well as having an enormous impact on the public. The word evolution simply means the "unfolding or orderly development of something." The theory of evolution, however, teaches much more than that, for it has far reaching implications in many fields of study. This theory, which was systematized and popularized by Charles Darwin in the 19th century, attempts to explain the way all life has come to be in its present form.

Life Developed By Chance

The general theory of evolution teaches that planet earth suddenly appeared about 5 billion years ago. About 1.5 to 2 billion years after earth appeared, life began to spring forth. On the earth was a primeval ocean in which primitive single-cell organisms developed by chance. Through mutation, chance variation, and natural selection, these single-celled creatures evolved over millions of years into fish. The fish, in turn, gave rise to amphibians, which evolved into reptiles. One line of reptiles gave rise to birds and another line to mammals.

Finally, man developed from a common ancestor with the ape. The plant kingdom, somewhere along the line, developed distinctly from the animal kingdom.

The theory of organic evolution teaches that all life, plants, animals, and man gradually developed over millions of years by natural processes from an original single cell. Spontaneous generation, which caused life to arise from non-life, happened only once and does not happen now.

The theory of evolution explains things in terms of processes that are still continuing to the present. Thus, evolution can be studied as an ongoing process.

Development Without God

The theory of evolution explains life without appealing to God or the supernatural. Julian Huxley explains:

In the evolutionary pattern of thought there is no longer either need or room for the supernatural. The earth was not created: it evolved. So did all of the animals and plants that inhabit it, including our human selves, mind and soul, as well as brain and body. So did religion. All aspects of reality are subject to evolution, from atoms and stars to fish and flowers . . . to human societies and values indeed . . . All reality is a single process of evolution (Julian Huxley, *Essays of a Humanist,* New York, Penguin: 1966, p. 128).

Michael Denton writes:

It was because Darwinian theory broke man's link with God and set him adrift in a cosmos without purpose or end that its impact was so fundamental. No other intellectual revolution (with the possible exception of the Copernican) so profoundly affected the way men view themselves and their place in the universe (Michael Denton, *Evolution: A Theory in Crisis,* Bethesda, Maryland: Adler and Adler, 1985, p. 67).

Accepted As Fact

The theory of evolution is accepted as fact in many places today. The late well-known evolutionist Theodosius Dobzhansky wrote:

The occurrence of the evolution of life in the history of the earth is established about as well as events not witnessed by human observers can be (T. Dobzhansky, *Science,* 127:1091, 1958).

Most textbooks, as well as popular writings, treat evolution not as a theory, but as a fact. Consider the following statements from Time-Life Books:

That foundation is evolution, the concept that there is a kinship among all forms of life because it evolved in an amplitude of time from one common ancestry, and that there are differences between them because they have diverged from that ancestry in taking over the earth, its air and its waters. Darwin did not invent the concept. But when he started his career, the doctrine of special creation could be doubted only by heretics. When he finished, the fact of evolution could be denied only by the abandonment of reason. He demolished the old theory with two books . . . *On the Origin of Species* . . . *The Descent of Man* (Ruth Moore, *Evolution,* New York: Time-Life Books, Time, Inc., 1962, p. 10).

Macroevolution

Evolution generally means a process of change in a certain direction. When we refer to evolution in the history of earthly life, we mean life as we know it today has come through a process of development from simple to more complex, "lower" to "higher" forms of life. These beneficial changes produce order and complexity in the different life forms. Evolutionists believe this process is still happening. Major changes from one species to another, or changes in other major categories of organisms is often referred to as macroevolution.

Microevolution

Scientists also use the term evolution to refer to individual variations within a "family" grouping or particular species. Those smaller changes are often referred to as microevolution.

Microevolution, or micromutation, can be defined as a small change in a plant or animal. This can be in size, change, or color. There is a considerable amount of evidence that microevolution occurs. This does not, however, contradict biblical teaching, for the Bible, as we shall see, allows for plants and animals to adapt and change. Evidence for microevolution is not evidence for macroevolution.

Cannot Be Proven Scientifically

Scientific proof calls for repetition, observation, and the possibility of falsification. The theory of evolution cannot be repeated, observed or falsified. It is beyond the realm of the experimental scientific method.

Too Slow

The evolution model demands that change took place over a long period of time. From the original primeval sea until the present, a time span of tens of millions of years have elapsed. Even though the processes are supposedly still going on, they are too slow to observe. This puts it out of the realm of scientific proof. The evolutionary scientist Dobzhansky wrote:

> These evolutionary happenings are unique, unrepeatable and irreversible. It is impossible to turn a land vertebrate into a fish as it is to effect the reverse transformation. The applicability of the experimental method to the study of such unique historical processes is severely restricted . . . by the time intervals involved, which far exceeds the lifetime of any human experimenter (T. Dobzhansky, *American Science*, 45:388, 1957).

Macroevolution must be accepted on faith. Evolution, at least in the sense that Darwin speaks of it, cannot be detected within the lifetime of a single observer.

Unfalsifiable

Another major problem with the theory of evolution is that in practice it is unfalsifiable. John Moore writes:

No matter what is observed, there usually is an appropriate evolutionary explanation for it. If an organ or organism develops, it has positive survival value; if it degenerates, it has negative survival value. If a complex biological system appears suddenly, it is due to preadaptation. 'Living fossils' (contemporary representatives of organisms expected to be extinct) survive because the environment did not change. If the environment changes and an evolutionary lineage survives, it is due to adaptation. If the lineage dies, it is because the environment changed too much, etc. Hence the concept cannot be falsified (John Moore, *How To Teach Origins*, Milford, Michigan: Mott Media, 1983, p. 47).

Gaps

There is also the matter of major gaps for which the theory of evolution has no clear explanation. Emery Bancroft writes:

1. The first and greatest gap which confronts the evolutionist is that between the living and non-living. The entire world of living creatures is assumed to have emerged, sometime and somehow, through "resident forces," out of the inorganic realm. Yet no trace of this marvelous process remains, and the inorganic world exhibits no progressiveness at all, no power or disposition to advance one hair's breadth.

2. The next gap is that between the vegetable and animal kingdoms. If the latter, in its entirety, arose out of the former through gradual and infinitesimal changes, no trace of that marvelous development remains; nor can there be found in the vegetable kingdom anything from which the characteristic features of animal life could have evolved.

3. Next we encounter the great gap between the vertebrates and the invertebrates; then between the mammals and other vertebrates; then the gaps between each of the million or so distinct species of organisms and every other; and finally the immense gap between man and the highest of the brutes.

In considering these great gaps, and the many lesser ones, it should be borne in mind that evolution is set forth expressly as a theory of origins, that is to say, as an explanation of how all the infinite varieties of things, living and non-living, came into existence. But origins, including those of the very broadest kind, are just what the theory conspicuously fails to explain. The evolutionist makes no pretense that his theory can explain the origin of either matter or force. The existence of these he must take for granted, attributing them to an unknowable First Cause (Emery H. Bancroft, *Christian Theology*, Grand Rapids: Zondervan, 2nd Revised edition, 1961, pp. 184,185).

Charles V. Taylor notes:

Evolution is in the peculiar position that it:

* has no way of observing significant, species-changing mutations of the past
* has no way of observing cataclysmic past events
* cannot apply present laboratory experiments to the past, a process sometimes known as 'extrapolation'
* has no written records to support changes in organisms, which are crucial to the support of its theories.

(Charles V. Taylor, *The Oldest Science Book in the World*, Slacks Creek, Queensland, Australia: Assembly Press, Pty. Ltd., 1984, pp. 128,129).

Evolution Requires Great Faith

Accepting the theory of evolution requires an inordinate amount of faith. Dr. R. L. Wysong comments:

Evolution requires plenty of faith: a faith in L-proteins that defy chance formation; a faith in the formation of the DNA codes which if generated spontaneously would spell only pandemonium; a faith in a primitive environment that in reality would fiendishly devour any chemical precursors to life; a faith in experiments that prove nothing but the need for intelligence in the beginning; a faith in a primitive ocean that would not thicken but would only hopelessly dilute chemicals; a faith in natural laws including the laws of thermodynamics and biogenesis that actually deny the possibility for the spontaneous generation of life; a faith in future scientific revelations that when realized always seem to present more dilemmas to the evolutionist; a faith in probabilities that treasonously tell two stories— one denying evolution, the other confirming the creator; faith in transformations that remain fixed; faith in mutations and natural selection; faith in fossils that embarrassingly show fixity through time, regular absence of transitional forms . . . a faith in time which proves to only promote degradation in the absence of mind; and faith in reductionism that ends up reducing the materialist's arguments to zero and forcing the need to invoke a supernatural Creator (R.L. Wysong, *The Creation-Evolution Controversy*, Midland, Michigan: Inquiry Press, 1981, p. 455).

Evolutionists Inconsistent

David Rosevear notes the inconsistent and illogical thinking of evolutionists:

In 1990 the Hubble Telescope was launched into orbit and began to send back pictures to earth from space. One of the declared aims of the project was to look for other planets outside our solar system, and to try to find extra-terrestrial life. How are we to recognize signs of life? We must look for coded messages by scanning the sky at various frequencies to try to pick up intelligent signals. The signals would have a non-random sequence (a design) and would carry information. Design and information are recognized as the product of intelligent life. Yet here on earth we look at the simplest cell, with its incredible miniaturized design and information, and wonder if it could somehow have arisen by chance! The reason for this double standard is that scientists, like other mortals, look for evidence which will support their philosophical world-view. If life has evolved on earth by chance, then surely it has evolved in many other places in this vast universe. While it is recognized that intelligent life-forms would send non-random messages, it is not accepted that non random sequences in genetic material here on earth can only be the product of an intelligent Designer. Evolutionism is not so much a science, more a philosophical world-view, with all the dogmatic assertions of religion (David Rosevear, *Creation Science*, Chichester, England: New Wine Press, 1991, p. 43).

Charles Darwin And The Evidence

A final point that should be raised concerning the theory of evolution concerns the man whose name is equated with it— Charles Darwin. It is important to note that Darwin was not drawn to the theory of evolution so much by the evidence, as he was desiring to reject the biblical account of creation. Robert Clark and James Bales write:

> There are some who think that Darwin accepted the theory of evolution only after many, many years of studying the subject. This, however is not the case. As his religious faith ebbed his faith in evolution developed. It came to fill up the void that was being left by his rejection of creation (Robert Clark and James D. Bales, *Why Scientists Accept Evolution*, Grand Rapids: Baker Book House, 1966, p. 35).

Problems Recognized

Darwin recognized the problems his theory had with the evidence. Two particular things bothering him were: (1) the fossil record, and (2) complicated organisms, such as the eye, that seemed to show design.

Fossil Record

If the theory of evolution is true, we should expect to find evidence of fish evolving into amphibia, reptiles to birds, a common ancestor with apes and man, etc. There should be literally millions of these transitional forms if evolution occurred as Darwin believed. The theory of evolution, therefore, can be demonstrated to be correct if this evidence is found in the fossil record. At Darwin's time the fossil record did not show this. He wrote:

> As by this theory, innumerable transitional forms must have existed. Why do we not find them imbedded in the crust of the earth? Why is all nature not in confusion instead of being as we see them, well-defined species? Geological research does not yield the infinitely many fine gradiation between past and present species required by the theory; and this is the most obvious of many objections which may be argued against it. The explanation lies, however, in the extreme imperfection of the geological record (Charles Darwin, *The Origin of Species*, Vol. 2, 6th Ed., p. 49).

When Darwin proposed his theory of evolution he realized the fossil record did not support it. He believed that once the fossil record was uncovered it would support his theory. The fossil record is no longer incomplete as it was in Darwin's day and it reveals that his idea of a gradual evolution is wrong!

Dr. David Raup, Dean of the Field Museum of Natural History in Chicago, observed:

> Well, we are now about 120 years after Darwin and the knowledge of the fossil record has been greatly expanded. We now have a quarter of a million fossil species but the situation hasn't changed much. The record of evolution is still surprisingly jerky and, ironically, we have fewer examples of evolutionary transition than we had in Darwin's time. By this I mean that some of the classic cases of Darwinian change in the fossil record, such as the evolution of the horse in North America, have had to be discarded or modified as a result of more detailed

information—what appears to be a nice simple progression when relatively few data were available now appears to be much more complex and much less gradualistic. So Darwin's problem has not been alleviated in the last 120 years and we still have a record which does show change but one that can hardly be looked upon as the most reasonable consequence of natural selection (David M. Raup, "Conflicts Between Darwin and Paleontology," Field Museum of Natural History Bulletin, Vol. 50, No. 1, Jan. 1979, p. 15).

Scientist Luther Sunderland asked Dr. Colin Patterson, a senior paleontologist at the British Museum (Natural History), why no evolutionary transitions were included in his book *Evolution*. Dr. Patterson replied:

I fully agree with your comments on the lack of direct illustration of evolutionary transitions in my book. If I knew of any, fossil or living, I would certainly have included them. You suggest that an artist should be asked to visualize such transformations, but where would he get the information from? I could not, honestly, provide it, and if I were to leave it to artistic license would it not mislead the reader? . . . Gould and the American Museum people are hard to contradict when they say that there are no transitional fossils. As a paleontologist myself, I am much occupied with the philosophical problems of identifying ancestral forms in the fossil record. You say that I should at least 'show a photo of the fossil from which each type of organism was derived.' I will lay it on the line—there is not one such fossil for which one could make a watertight argument (Dr. Colin Patterson in a personal letter to Luther D. Sunderland, April 10, 1979).

The fossil record continues to be a major source of embarrassment for evolutionists.

Design

Darwin was also bothered by organisms, such as the human eye, that seemed to show intricate design. He did not have an explanation how it could all happen by chance. Evolutionary critic Francis Hitching writes:

> Now it is quite evident that if the slightest thing goes wrong en route—if the cornea is fuzzy, or the pupil fails to dilate, or the lens becomes opaque, or the focussing goes wrong—then a recognizable image is not formed. The eye either functions as a whole, or not at all. So how did it come to evolve by slow, steady, infinitesimally small Darwinian improvements? Is it really possible that thousands upon thousands of lucky chance mutations happened coincidentally so that the lens and the retina, which cannot work without each other, evolved in synchrony? What survival value can there be in an eye that doesn't see? Small wonder that it troubled Darwin. 'To this day it makes me shudder,' he wrote to his botanist friend Asa Gray in February, 1890 (Francis Hitching, *The Neck of the Giraffe*, London: Pan Publishers, 1982, pp. 85,86).

Other examples could be given. The point is that Darwin did not embrace evolution because of indisputable evidence. On the contrary, he realized that the evidence contradicted his theory, yet he held it anyway. This again illustrates that it is not because of clearcut evidence that people hold on to the idea of mindless evolution.

Summary

In our brief overview we have seen that the theory of evolution attempts to explain the development of life from a single cell until the present complex universe. This evolution, or change, took millions of years to occur. The theory of evolution explains man and the universe apart from the need for God.

The theory of evolution, which is generally accepted as fact in the scientific world, cannot be proven scientifically. Furthermore, there are great problems with the theory when compared to the facts of science. Darwin saw some of these problems and had no answer for them. Thus, the evolutionist must believe the theory because of faith, not because of compelling scientific evidence.

14

WHAT ARE THE CONSEQUENCES OF ACCEPTING THE THEORY OF EVOLUTION?

The theory of atheistic evolution is not limited to biological concepts. If the theory of evolution is correct then it has far reaching consequences for the Christian faith as well as for all of humanity. The following are some of the logical results of accepting the modern atheistic theory of evolution:

1. There is no God.

2. The Bible is wrong.

3. Life arose by chance.

4. There is no need for a Savior.

5. There is no basis of right or wrong.

6. Mankind has no genuine hope for the future.

1. No God Exists

The theory of evolution lies at the root of many belief systems that reject the idea of God and the supernatural. Humanism, for example, rejects the idea of a Creator God and embraces the theory of evolution. Hence, the Humanist Manifesto declares the following in its first two affirmations:

Affirmation 1: Religious Humanists regard the universe as self-existing and not created.

Affirmation 2: Humanism believes that man is a part of nature and that he has emerged as a result of a continuous process.

Humanist faith rests in the theories of Charles Darwin. Dr. Colin Patterson of the British Museum of Natural History said:

Just as Pre-Darwinian biology was carried out by people whose faith was in the creator and his plan, post-Darwinian biology is being carried out by people whose faith is in, almost, the deity of Darwin (quoted in "Are the Reports of Darwin's Death Exaggerated?" by Brian Leith, *The Listener*, Vol. 106, No. 2370, October 8, 1981, p. 390).

Though not all evolutionists are atheists, evolution taken to its logical conclusion does not require a Creator. According to the theory of evolution, everything that now exists is a result of chance and natural processes.

Hence, if the atheistic theory of evolution is true, then the God of Scripture, who tells us He created the universe by His power, does not exist.

2. The Bible Is Wrong

The Bible teaches that God is the Creator of the universe. In contrast, the theory of evolution holds that we are here by chance, not by design. If the theory of evolution is true, then the Bible is wrong. One evolutionary writer put it this way:

Here is a theory that released thinking men from the spell of superstition, one of the most overpowering that has ever enslaved mankind . . . We owe to the *Origin of Species* the overthrow of the myth of creation (C. Darlington, "Origin of Evolution," *Scientific American*, May, 1959, p. 60).

Any claim that the Bible is the authoritative inerrant Word of God would be refuted if the theory of evolution is correct.

The logical result of accepting evolution is a denial of the plain teachings of Scripture, as Sir Cecil Wakeley, past president of the Royal College of Surgeons, admitted:

The theory of evolution is the gospel of the atheist and paves the way to the complete rejection of the Bible ("A Surgeon Looks At Evolution," cited by the Evolution Protest Movement, No. 223, January, 1980).

3.   Life Is Here By Chance

Even though the evolutionist seeks to exclude the supernatural from scientific discussions, in many ways he does have a god. The god of the evolutionist is the god of chance. As we have seen, it requires more faith to believe that the god of chance could accomplish the bringing about of the universe in all its form and complexity than to believe it has been brought about by the wisdom and planning of the God of the Bible.

If the theory of evolution is the correct explanation of the development of life on earth, then we are here by chance. The universe came into existence due to an explosion of some dense particle of unknown origin and life on earth came into existence due to the spontaneous generation of life at the sub-microscopic level.

Nobel prize-winning chemist Jacque Monod wrote in his book *Chance and Necessity*:

Pure chance, absolutely free but blind, is at the very root of the stupendous edifice of evolution.

The agnostic Monod compared the initial formation of life to playing a roulette wheel. He further wrote:

> The universe was not pregnant with life or the biosphere with man. Our number came up in a Monte Carlo game. Is it surprising that, like the person who has just made a million at the casino, we should feel strange and a little unreal?

Scientist Richard Leakey concurs:

> We are here as a result of a series of accidents, if you like. There was nothing preplanned about humanity (Richard Leakey, "The Making of Mankind I," *The Listener*, May 7, 1981, p. 598).

Love?

The theory of evolution also reduces love to mere chemical reactions. Robert Wright notes:

> Love itself—the love of a mother for child, husband for wife, sibling for sibling—may boil down, in large part, to a chemical called oxytocin. It seems somehow harder to rhapsodize about the universal love so many religions prescribe when you know that, if it ever comes, it will rest on the same stuff researchers inject into rats to make them cuddle. Another bit of less-than-inspiring news is the clearer more cynical, understanding of why love exists— how it was designed by evolution for only one discernible purpose: to spread the genes of the person doing the loving (Robert Wright, "Science, God, and Man," *Time*, December 28, 1992, p. 40).

4.   No Need For A Savior

If the theory of evolution is true then the coming of Jesus Christ is unnecessary. The Bible says Jesus Christ came to die for the sins of the world:

Just as the Son of Man did not come to be served, but to serve, and to give His life a ransom for many (Matthew 20:28).

John the Baptist recognized that Jesus' mission was to take away the world's sin:

The next day John saw Jesus coming and said, 'Behold! the Lamb of God who takes away the sin of the world' (John 1:29).

This is necessary because the Scripture says man is separated from God by his sin:

For all have sinned and come short of the glory of God (Romans 3:23).

Sin will cause physical death and eventual eternal separation from God. The Bible says:

The wages of sin is death (Romans 6:23).

Atheists recognize the theory of evolution strips Christianity of any meaning. Atheist G. Richard Bozarth writes:

Christianity has fought, still fights and will fight science to the desperate end over evolution, because evolution destroys utterly and finally the very reason Jesus' earthly life was supposedly made necessary. Destroy Adam and Eve and the original sin, and in the rubble you will find the sorry remains of the son of god . . . If Jesus is not the redeemer who died for our sins, and this is what evolution means, then Christianity is nothing (G. Richard Bozarth, "The Meaning of Evolution," *The American Atheist,* Vol. 20, No. 2, February, 1978, p. 30).

If evolution is true, mankind is not answerable to God and has no need for a Savior. Consequently, Jesus Christ would not be what He claimed to be—the Savior of the world and mankind's only hope.

5. No Distinction Between Right Or Wrong

If indeed there is no Creator, then we are left without any moral absolutes, without anyone to answer. The logical result of rejecting a Creator and His moral absolutes is to accept that all things are now conceivable. There is no moral anchor to guide us. Thus, to make statements such as "murder is wrong" or "loving is right" is entirely meaningless because there is no one to say what is right and what is wrong.

The French philosopher John Paul Sartre realized this and wrote:

> I was like a man who lost his shadow. And there was nothing left in heaven, no right or wrong, nor anyone to give me orders . . . I am doomed to have no other law but mine . . . For I, Zeus, am a man and every man must find his own way (John Paul Sartre, "The Flies in Sartre," *No Exit and Other Plays*, New York: Vintage Books, 1946, pp. 121-123).

Sartre also wrote:

> All human activities are equivalent . . . Thus it amounts to the same thing whether one gets drunk alone or is a leader of a nation (John Paul Sartre, *Being And Nothingness*, New York: Philosophical Library, 1956, p. 766).

Man now creates his own destiny; he is the master of his own fate. Jeremy Rifkin wrote:

> We no longer feel ourselves to be guests in someone else's home and therefore obliged to make our behavior conform with a set of preexisting cosmic rules. It is our creation now. We make the rules. We establish the parameters of reality. We create the world, and because we do, we no longer feel beholden to outside forces. We no longer have to justify our behavior, for we are now the architects of the universe. We are responsible to nothing outside ourselves, for we are the kingdom, the power, and the glory forever and ever (Jeremy Rifkin, *Algeny*, New York: Viking Press, 1983, p. 188).

If we evolved by mere chance, then there is no one out there to tell us how to live.

6. No Hope

Finally, if the theory of evolution is true and mankind is here by chance, then there is no purpose for our existence. Hope, then, is merely an illusion. The rejection of a Creator God leads an individual to hopelessness and despair. Russell Kirk observes:

> To practical men and women in this work-a-day world, do these questions of the origin of the universe, the earth's environment, and mankind make any real difference? Cannot such abstract disputations be resigned to preachers and professors?
> No they cannot. For upon the questions about origins depend the answers of whether life is worth living and how it is to be lived . . . The bent condition of human existence in these closing decades of the 20th century is an affliction resulting principally from the decay of belief in an ordered universe and in a purpose for human existence (Russell Kirk, "The Rediscovery of Creation," *National Review*, May 27, 1983, p. 616).

Logically, if one accepts evolution, then genuine hope for the future does not exist.

Summary

The acceptance of the theory of evolution has far-reaching ramifications for humanity. If the biblical answer is not true, then the God of the Bible does not exist, the Bible is incorrect, mankind is an accident with no need for a Savior, and we are without any moral absolutes or realistic hope for the future. Belief in evolution undermines the entire Christian faith.

Fortunately, we have an intelligent alternative to the theory of evolution—special creation.

15

WHAT IS THE BIBLICAL ACCOUNT OF SPECIAL CREATION?

The Bible says that the universe was brought into existence through a series of creative acts by an all-powerful, loving God. The Scriptures clearly teach that God is the Creator of all things.

The concept of creation is not an obscure doctrine in the Scriptures. There are at least one hundred references in the Bible referring to God's creative activity. It is the first doctrine to be stated:

In the beginning God created the heavens and the earth (Genesis 1:1).

Creation is also one of the last to be restated:

You are worthy, O Lord, to receive glory and honor and power; for You created all things, and by Your will they exist and were created (Revelation 4:11).

The fact that God made the heaven and the earth is taken for granted by the biblical writers. Furthermore, the Bible assumes the creation account as literally having occurred.

There is no hint in Scripture that it is to be taken as poetry or as an allegory.

The biblical account of creation teaches the following things about man and the universe.

Creation Was Supernatural

The account of creation recorded in the Bible is a supernatural work of God. The Lord says:

> I am the Lord, who makes all things, who stretches out the heavens all alone (Isaiah 44:24).

Creation was accomplished by the Word of the Lord,

> By the word of the Lord the heavens were made, and all the host of them by the breath of His mouth. He gathers the waters of the sea together as a heap . . . For He spoke, and it was done; He commanded and it stood fast (Psalm 33:6,7,9).

God gives a challenge to those who would attempt to give their account of the origin of the universe:

> Where were you when I laid the foundations of the earth? Tell me if you have understanding. Who determined its measurements? Surely you know (Job 38:4,5).

Out Of Nothing

Scripture further indicates that God created the universe out of no pre-existing materials. The word translated "create" in Genesis 1:1 is the Hebrew word *bara.* God is always the subject when this verb is used. The verb *bara* is used for creating out of nothing in Genesis 1:1, and in most other places it appears in the Bible.

In addition, the New Testament makes it clear that God created the universe by His spoken Word alone:

> By faith we understand that the worlds were framed by the word of God, so that the things which are seen were

not made of things which are visible (Hebrews 11:3).

Hence, with regard to physical entities there were no pre-existent materials used. Man, however, was made from the dust of the earth that God had previously created.

One of the modern theories that attempts to explain the origin of the universe teaches that matter is eternal. The Bible refutes the idea of the eternity of matter by stating that God created the world out of nothing. That the God of the Bible has the ability to create something from nothing can be summed up in a rhetorical question God asked the prophet Jeremiah:

Behold, I am the Lord, the God of all flesh. Is there anything too hard for Me? (Jeremiah 32:27).

Perfect

After each act of creation, God pronounced it good. When God finished creating the heavens and the earth they were perfect:

Then God saw everything that He had made, and indeed it was very good (Genesis 1:31).

There was no imperfection in God's original creation. Imperfection eventually entered the universe as a result of mankind's sin, not God's design. Thus, the universe as it exists today is not the same as God created it. Sin has brought into it abnormality and imperfection.

Details Of Creation

Scripture gives various details of the creation narrative. God has counted the stars and given them all names:

He counts all the number of stars; He calls them all by name (Psalm 147:4).

Scripture speaks of God creating the elements:

For He looks to the ends of the earth, and sees under the whole heavens, to establish a weight for the wind, and mete out waters by measure. When He made a law for the rain, and a path for the thunderbolt (Job 28:24-26).

It is God who created the heavenly bodies:

Do you know the balance of the clouds, those wondrous works of Him who is perfect in knowledge . . . With Him, have you spread out the skies, strong as a cast metal mirror? (Job 37:16,18).

The day is Yours, the night also is yours; You have prepared the light and the sun. You have set all the borders of the earth; You have made summer and winter (Psalm 74:16).

Jeremiah records the limitlessness of creation:

As the host of heaven cannot be numbered, nor the sand of the sea measured (Jeremiah 33:22).

The prophet Amos speaks of the creation of constellations:

He made Pleiades and Orion; He turns the shadow of death into morning and makes the day dark as night; He calls for the waters of the sea and pours them out on the face of the earth; the Lord is His name (Amos 5:8).

The Bible contrasts the changelessness of God with an ever-changing creation:

Of old You have laid the foundation of the earth, and the heavens are the work of Your hands. They will perish, but You will endure; yes all of them will grow old like a garment; like a cloak You will change them, and they will be changed. But You are the same, and Your years will have no end (Psalm 102:25-27).

Creation And Preservation

The Bible says that God not only created the universe He is also presently preserving it. Creation is dependent upon God. The prophet Nehemiah wrote:

You alone are the Lord; You have made heaven, the heaven of heavens, with all their host, the earth and all things on it, the seas and all that is in them, and you preserve them all. The host of heaven worships You (Nehemiah 9:6).

Jeremiah commented:

He had made the earth by His power; He has established the world by His wisdom, and stretched out the heaven by His understanding. When He utters His voice—there is a multitude of waters in the heavens; he causes the vapors of earth to ascend from the ends of the earth; He make lightning for the rain; He brings the wind out of His treasuries (Jeremiah 51:15,16).

Days

There was a division of the creative activity into days. In the Old Testament the usual meaning of the Hebrew word for day, *yom*, is a twenty-four hour day. The days have usually been understood to be solar days, though there are other ways in which they may be viewed. As to the various ways we may understand the days of Genesis see my book *Understanding the Early Chapters of Genesis* (Spokane, Washington: AusAmerica Publishers, 1993).

New Testament

The New Testament gives reference to God as Creator. On Mars Hill the Apostle Paul said:

God, made the world and everything in it, since He is Lord of heaven and earth, does not dwell in temples made with hands. Nor is He worshiped with men's hands, as though He needed anything, since He gives to all life, breath, and all things (Acts 17:24,25).

John the Apostle writes:

You are worthy, O Lord, to receive glory and honor and power; for you have created all things, and by Your will they exist and were created (Revelation 4:11).

The Apostle Paul says the creation gives the atheist no excuse:

For since the creation of the world His invisible attributes are clearly seen, being understood by things that are made, even His eternal power and Godhead, so that they are without excuse (Romans 1:20).

When Paul wrote to the church at Corinth he refers to God commanding the light to appear in Genesis 1:3:

For it is the God who commanded light to shine out of darkness who has shown in our hearts (2 Corinthians 4:6).

Peter makes reference to Genesis 1:9:

For this they willfully forget; that by the word of God the heavens were of old, and the earth standing out of water and in the water (2 Peter 3:5).

Supernatural creation is an important truth that is emphasized in both testaments.

Testimony Of Jesus

We have already seen that the Scriptures testify that Jesus is the Creator. Last, but certainly not least, we have the testimony of Jesus Himself as to the creation account in Genesis.

Have you not read that He who made them at the beginning made them male and female, and said, 'For this reason a man shall leave his father and mother and be

joined to his wife, and the two shall become one flesh'?
(Matthew 19:4,5).

Jesus quotes Genesis 1:27 and 2:24, which demonstrates that
He believed God created Adam and Eve in the beginning.

If Jesus is the One whom He claimed to be, God the Son,
then His testimony settles the issue. His Word is the final
authority on every issue.

Summary

The following conclusions can be drawn from what the Bible
says about creation:

1. The Scriptures give many references to the doctrine
   of creation. It is by no means something obscure.

2. God is assumed to be the Creator of heaven and earth.
   There are no arguments in Scripture given to prove it. His
   existence is accepted as a fact.

3. Creation was regarded as a historical event. There is no
   indication that the Scripture writers considered the
   story a myth.

4. There are many references outside of Genesis that add
   details to the creation narrative.

5. Scripture also teaches that creation was out of
   nothing—no preexistent materials.

6. Finally, and most importantly, Jesus testified to the fact
   that God created the heavens and the earth.

Ultimately, the Christian believes what God has revealed
about creation because it has been recorded in His Word, the
Bible. Though there was no human being present when it
happened, God the Father, God the Son, and God the Holy
Spirit, were there. Though not all details are included in the
record, many facts are, and they should be understood in the

same way as other Scriptures. Hence, the biblical account of creation recorded in Genesis should be accepted as what actually happened in the beginning.

16

WHAT DOES BIBLICAL CREATIONISM TEACH US ABOUT THE NATURE OF GOD?

The biblical teaching on creation refutes four popular "isms:" atheism, polytheism, pantheism, and deism. All of these views are contradicted by what the Bible has to say about God's creative activity.

Atheism

The biblical account of creation refutes atheism because Scripture maintains the existence of an all-powerful God. The existence of God is assumed in Scripture; the Bible never attempts to prove He exists.

Scripture says that God is Spirit:

God is Spirit, and those who worship Him must worship in spirit and truth (John 4:24).

As such He is the invisible God:

Now to the King eternal, immortal, invisible, to God, who alone is wise, be honor and glory forever and ever. Amen (1 Timothy 1:17).

No one has seen Him:

No one has seen God at any time. The only begotten Son, who is in the bosom of the Father, He has declared Him (John 1:18).

Who alone has immortality, dwelling in unapproachable light, who no man has seen or can see (1 Timothy 6:16).

A spirit has no physical form:

Behold, My hands and My feet, that it is I myself. Handle Me and see, for a spirit does not have flesh and bones as you see I have (Luke 24:39).

Yet the universe that God created is both material and visible, and as such reflects His power and majesty.

Polytheism

Creation also refutes polytheism, the belief in many gods, by stating that only one God exists and creates. The Bible is clear that although there be other so-called gods, there is only one eternal God who exists:

'You are my witnesses,' says the Lord, 'and my servants whom I have chosen, that you may know and believe Me, and understand that I am He, before Me there was no God formed, nor shall there be after Me' (Isaiah 43:10).

Though the Bible makes reference to false gods, it does not state that these are actual gods who exist. The Apostle Paul wrote:

But, then indeed, when you did not know God, you served those which by nature are not gods (Galatians 4:8).

Scripture shows that these false gods are not to be compared with the one true God:

To whom will you liken Me, and make Me equal and compare Me, that we should be alike? They lavish gold out of the bag, and weigh silver in the balance; they hire a goldsmith, and he makes it a god; they prostrate themselves, yes, they worship. They bear it on the shoulder, they carry it and set it in its place, and it stands; from its place it shall not move. Though one cries out to it, yet it cannot answer nor save him out of trouble (Isaiah 46:5-7).

These so-called gods were inventions in the mind of people who rejected the truth of the one true God. Only the God of the Bible has real substance.

Since the God of the Bible has given us reason to believe in His existence, whatever He might say on the matter of other gods is final. There are no other true gods. God says He is the only God who exists. That solves the question.

Pantheism

There is a view of God's nature known as pantheism. The term is derived from two Greek words *pan* and *theos*. *Pan* means "all or everything" and *theos* means "God." Pantheism, therefore, means "God is everything."

Pantheism teaches that everything that exists is part of one single reality and that reality is called god. God is all and all is god. There is no distinction between the creature and the creator in pantheism. God is equal to anything and everything. The concept of a personal God who created the universe as a separate substance is foreign to pantheism.

Scripture makes the distinction between the Creator and that which He created:

In the beginning God created the heavens and the earth (Genesis 1:1).

For since the creation of the world His invisible attributes are clearly seen, being understood by the things that are made, even His eternal power and Godhead (Romans 1:20).

The universe has not existed eternally but God has. When God created the universe He brought into being something different from Himself:

By faith we understand that the worlds were framed by the word of God, so that the things which are seen were not made of things which are visible (Hebrews 11:3).

Pantheism blurs this distinction. The God of the Bible is not the same god of pantheism because He is not the same thing as His physical universe. God is the artist and the physical universe is His masterpiece. It is wrong to worship the creation. The Book of Romans speaks of those who do:

Who exchanged the truth of God for the lie, and worshipped and served the creature rather than the Creator, who is blessed forever. Amen (Romans 1:25).

Worship of any other thing, living or dead, is condemned:

You shall not make for yourself any carved image, or any likeness of anything that is in heaven above, or that is in the earth beneath, or that is in the water under the earth (Exodus 20:4).

Deism

There are those that hold a view of God's nature called deism. Deism believes that God created the world, set it in motion, but then backed off. The god of deism does not play an active role in his world but allows the universe to run by natural and self-sustaining laws that He established. Although deists believe in a supernatural creation of the world, they do not believe in supernatural intervention in the world. Because there is no supernatural intervention by God, deists believe that miracles do not occur. Hence, they deny the miraculous accounts given in Scripture.

Deism is in contradiction to the God revealed in Scripture. If God can create the universe, as deists agree that He did, then He certainly is capable of performing other miracles of less magnitude. This is what the Bible says occurred. The Bible, from the first page until the last, is an account of God intervening miraculously in human history. To admit the miracle of creation, and then to deny other miracles, is an inconsistent position.

The deist position would have God as a master "clockmaker." He made the clock, wound it, then left it alone. But the Bible portrays God as much more than a great "clockmaker." He is a loving Father who is personally interested in His children. God desires that humanity call out to Him when they have a need. God says:

> Call upon Me in the day of trouble; I will deliver you and you shall glorify Me (Psalm 50:15).

The deist position, that God created the universe but does not participate in the running of it, is contrary to what the Bible says.

God Of The Bible

The biblical position is that the creation was brought about by the God of the Bible—the only God who exists. In both the Old and New Testaments it is clear that there is only one God. The prophet Isaiah records God saying:

> Before Me there was no God formed, nor shall there be after Me (Isaiah 43:10).

In the New Testament the Apostle Paul tells Timothy:

> For there is one God (1 Timothy 2:5).

God Is A Trinity

In Genesis 1:1 the word translated God is the Hebrew word *Elohim*. It is a uniplural noun (meaning 3 or more) but is used with a singular verb. Within the nature of the one God there are three distinct personalities. They are named the Father, the Son, and the Holy Spirit. These three personalities are co-equal and co-eternal. They constitute the one God; this is known as the Trinity. Although the Scriptures do not explain how the one God can be three separate persons, it does clearly teach it. For further references on the doctrine of the Trinity see Don Stewart, *What Everyone Needs To Know About God*, Spokane, Washington: AusAmerica Publishers, 1992.

The Trinity Involved In Creation

We have already noted that the Bible teaches that creation was an act of God. As we search the Scriptures we find that creation was completed by all three members of the Trinity: God the Father, God the Son, and God the Holy Spirit.

God The Father

Scripture testifies that God the Father was the Designer, Architect and Planner of creation. Speaking of God the Father, Jesus said:

But from the beginning of creation God made them male and female (Mark 10:6).

In another place He said:

For in those days there will be tribulation, such as has not been from the beginning of creation which God created until this time (Mark 13:19).

Jesus believed and taught that God the Father was involved in creation.

Jesus Was The Creator

Jesus Christ is recognized in Scripture as the Creator of the universe:

All things were made through Him, and without Him nothing was made that was made (John 1:3).

Here we have the statement that everything was created by Jesus. Not one thing has been created apart from Him.

The Apostle Paul also testifies to Jesus as the Creator:

> For by Him all things were created that are in heaven and that are on earth, visible and invisible, whether thrones or dominions or principalities or powers. All things were created through Him and for Him (Colossians 1:16).

This statement makes it abundantly clear that Jesus created all things in the universe.

Sustains The Creation

Not only did Jesus create everything in the beginning, He also sustains His creation. The Apostle Paul, after testifying to the creative work of Jesus, writes:

> And He is before all things, and in Him all things hold together (Colossians 1:16 NASB).

Jesus is the one who holds the universe together. He is the one who keeps it running in an orderly fashion.

The Book of Hebrews takes this a step further. It teaches that Christ is "upholding all things by the word of His power" (Hebrews 1:3). The idea is that Jesus is keeping all things together by His spoken word. Thus, it is the spoken word of Jesus that now upholds the universe.

Jesus Christ created the universe, He sustains it by His spoken word, and He also rules it. The Apostle Paul testified that Christ is "the head over all rule and authority" (Colossians 2:10 NASB). The universe and all that is in it is ruled by Jesus.

The Holy Spirit As Creator

The Holy Spirit, the third member of the Trinity, was also involved in creating the universe. The psalmist writes:

> You send forth Your Spirit, they are created; and You renew the face of the earth (Psalm 104:30).

Job testifies:

By His Spirit He adorned the heavens (Job 26:13).

As was true with God the Father, and God the Son, God the Holy Spirit also participated in creation.

Conclusion

The biblical account of creation refutes atheism, polytheism, pantheism, and deism. We could also include naturalism, materialism, secularism, and agnosticism.

The Bible teaches that the three Persons of the Trinity, God the Father, God the Son, and God the Spirit were all involved in creating the universe. Creation, therefore, was accomplished by the one true God.

17

DOES THE BIBLE TEACH THE FIXITY OF THE SPECIES?

The Bible says the different animals and plants reproduced after their kind:

So God created great sea creatures and every living thing that moves, with which the waters abounded, according to their kind, and every winged bird according to its kind. And God saw that it was good (Genesis 1:21).

Some have taken this to mean that the Bible teaches the "fixity of the species," or the idea that God created every single species and that none of these species ever changed. It was this idea that turned Charles Darwin against the Bible.

In the Galapagos Islands off the coast of South America, Darwin observed species of animals and birds that closely resembled those on the mainland. However, they were not exactly identical. The discovery of different species led Darwin to believe that all of them had descended from a common pair. He further believed he had observed transitional types in which one species was changing into another. If this was true it would contradict what he had been taught about the "fixity of the species."

Not Biblical Teaching

The so-called fixity of the species, as Darwin perceived the Bible to be saying, is not taught in Scripture. In fact, it wasn't even widely taught in the church before the eighteenth century. Sylvia Baker writes:

> The idea that species cannot change was certainly not an article of the church before the eighteenth century. It was then considered quite in accord with the Bible to believe that they could change, though not in the direction of greater complexity. It was not until the eighteenth century that the view became widespread that species cannot change, that they are 'fixed or immutable.' The man responsible for promoting it was Linnaeus, who is famous as the first man to introduce systematics to biology. He maintained that species as he had defined them represented the 'kind' of the Bible and therefore could not be changed.
>
> This view became widely accepted, insisted on, and carried to absurd limits. At one time it was even taught that there were sixty species of man, each of which had been created separately! When Darwin made his observations in the Galapagos Islands, the idea that species could not change was both a scientific and theological dogma. When he observed the evidence that suggested they could change, Darwin said, 'It is like confessing a murder' (Slyvia Baker, *Bone of Contention,* Revised edition, Sunnybank, Queensland, Australia, Evangelical Press: 1976, p. 7).

The problem was a misunderstanding of what the Bible says. The word translated in Genesis as "kind" is the Hebrew word *min*. It cannot be equated with our modern term *species*. This can be observed from the following passage in the Book of Leviticus:

> The ostrich, the short-eared owl, the seagull, and the hawk after its kind: the little owl, the fisher owl and the screech owl (Leviticus 11:16,17).

From this passage we see that the Bible recognizes various types of owls, as well as various types of other species. Therefore, the biblical word "kind" is not limited to our modern term "species." There are many varieties of fish, plants, cattle, as well as men and women.

John Klotz comments further:

> We also need to recognize that the language of the Bible is the commonsense, everyday language of our newspapers. This language does not change; technical scientific language does change . . . . We may have new 'species' of tomatoes, but they are still the same 'kind.' There may be changes within the species, yet tomatoes have not developed into cantaloupes or watermelons. There may also have been changes within the dog 'kind,' but these have not developed into lions or bears (John Klotz, *Studies in Creation*, St. Louis: Concordia Publishing House, 1985, p. 76).

Hence, what Darwin discovered was not contradictory to what the Bible has to say about 'kinds.' The Bible teaches "the fixity of the species" in that each biblical kind can only reproduce within certain fixed boundaries. Change within a kind, however, is consistent with biblical teaching. Today, whenever kinds are crossed, the offspring is always sterile. For example, a donkey and a horse produce a sterile mule. A lion crossed with a tiger produces a sterile liger. Charles Darwin saw this problem and wrote in *The Origin of Species*.

> How can we account for species, when crossed, being sterile and producing sterile offspring, whereas, when varieties are crossed, their fertility is unimpaired?

There is still no answer to this question today if one accepts the evolution model.

Change Is Permissible

Often the creationist position is caricatured by stating flatly that creationists deny the fact of change. This is not true.

Scientist Gary Parker writes:

> When someone asks me if I believe in evolution, I'll often say, 'Why, yes, no, no, yes, no.' The answer really depends on what the person means by evolution. In one sense evolution means 'change.' Do I believe in change? Yes indeed—I've got some in my pocket.
>
> But change isn't the real question, of course, change is just as much a part of the creation model as the evolution model. The question is, what kind of change do we see: change only within type (creation) or change also from one type to another (evolution)? (Gary Parker, *What Is Creation Science?*, El Cajon, California, Master Books: 1982, p. 82).

Summary

The Bible allows for change or variations within plants and animals. Change is evidence for microevolution or selection. What creationists are denying is the existence of any evidence for macroevolution. They reject the procedure of using evidence for microevolution as confirming the theory of macroevolution. Unfortunately, a great many people believe that evidence for microevolution proves macroevolution. This is by no means the case.

Furthermore, the Bible limits the amount of change which can happen. Cats cannot mate with dogs, pigs with apes, etc. This limitation is exactly what we find in our world. Hence, the Bible is certainly not unscientific when its says that 'kinds' of plants and animals are limited in the degree in which they can change.

18

CAN BIBLICAL CREATIONISM BE PROVEN SCIENTIFICALLY?

Creationism, like the theory of evolution, cannot be scientifically proven. The creation model teaches that the universe was created once at a particular time in the past. The Bible says that God has ceased creating. Creation has been finished:

Thus the heavens and the earth, and all the host of them were finished. And on the seventh day God ended His work which He had done (Genesis 2:1,2).

Creation cannot be observed since it has already happened. One can only observe the effects of creation. John Moore writes:

The concept of creation does not appear to meet the criterion of falsifiability any better than evolution. Science is not at its best when dealing with unique past events, whether these be considered as evolution or creation. Therefore it is surprising to find a statement signed by more than 120 scientists stating that creationism is a 'purely religious view' while evolution is labeled as 'strictly scientific' (John N. Moore, *How To Teach Origins*, Milford, Michigan, Mott Media: 1983, p. 49).

Predictions

Although neither the theory of evolution nor special creation can be scientifically proven, predictions can be made as to what evidence we should expect to find based upon each theory. Henry Morris explains:

Clearly, neither model of origins—creation or evolution—is scientific in this sense. Neither one can be tested, for the simple reason that we cannot repeat history . . . That does not mean, however, that their results cannot be observed and tested. That is, we can define two 'models' of origins, and then make comparative predictions as to what our observations should find if evolution is true, and conversely, what we should find if creation is true. The model that enables us to do the best job of predicting things which we then find to be true on observation is the model most likely to be true, even though we cannot prove it to be true by actual scientific repetition (Henry Morris in *What Is Creation Science?*, with Gary Parker, El Cajon, Calif: Master Books, Revised edition, 1987, p. 9).

Design

Though not provable in the strict scientific sense, biblical creationists believe that their view makes more sense out of the available evidence. One of strongest pieces of evidence is that the world shows evidence of design.

Here is a simple illustration: Suppose a husband and wife are walking on the beach and come across a giant sand castle. This castle is very elaborately designed with considerable detail. The wife mentions to her husband the time and hard work it must have taken the person or persons to build it. However, the husband objects to her conclusion. He says it was not built by anyone but came about by a series of random forces such as waves and wind. He insists that the sand castle is merely a result of chance. Now who is right? Neither can prove his or her position. Neither observed the castle being formed and there is no experiment that can be performed to determine whether or not this castle was a result of chance or design. Each believes his position by faith. Though one explanation may be more reasonable than the other, neither can be proved. Why does the wife believe the sand castle was designed? Because it makes the most sense of the available facts.

The argument from design is consistent with the biblical teaching of a caring Designer.

Evidence Clearly Seen

The Bible says that the evidence for a Creator is clearly seen by all mankind:

> For since the creation of the world His invisible attributes are clearly seen, being understood by the things that are made, even His eternal power and Godhead, so that they are without excuse (Romans 1:20).

If the evidence is so clear, why don't more people acknowledge God as Creator? The Bible again has the answer:

> For the wrath of God is revealed from heaven against all ungodliness and unrighteousness of men, who suppress the truth in unrighteousness (Romans 1:18).

According to Scripture, the main reason people do not acknowledge God as Creator is because they do not wish to. It is not because they cannot see; it is because they *will* not see. They willingly suppress God's truth because they do not want to worship Him.

Summary

Biblical creationism, like the theory of evolution, cannot be proven scientifically. Yet everything we see in nature testifies to a caring Designer. The testimony for design in nature is there for all of us to see, yet it is only through the Scripture that we can know the identity of the Designer. Therefore, any argument given for design must combine the evidence from the world around us, as well as the testimony of Scripture.

19

WHAT IS
THEISTIC EVOLUTION?

Atheistic evolution leaves no room for God, for it explains all of existence through ongoing natural processes. There are those, however, who attempt to wed the theory of evolution with the teaching of special creation as recorded in the Bible. This idea is known as theistic evolution.

Many people who feel the Bible is not intended to convey any information about the universe also believe that the theory of evolution causes no problem for the Christian. God, they say, only tells us "that" He created the universe, but He did not tell us "how." Therefore, there exists a number of scientists who call themselves "Christian evolutionists" or "theistic evolutionists."

Theistic evolution covers a broad range of ideas. Generally, it takes the position that evolution happened, but that a Creator or intelligence was somehow involved in the process. Most theistic evolutionists believe in some direct acts of a Creator. There is a difference regarding the number and the extent of the Creator's direct acts. Writer Batsell Barrett Baxter provides a working definition of theistic evolution:

The theistic evolutionist holds a position somewhat between that of the absolute evolutionist and the creationist. He believes that God created the materials of our universe and then guided and superintended the process by which all life has evolved from the very simplest one-celled form on up to the sophisticated forms which we know today. Evolution was God's method of bringing about the present development though originally the materials were created by God (Batsell Barrett Baxter, *I Believe Because,* Grand Rapids, Baker Book House: 1971, p. 159).

The Case For Theistic Evolution

Theistic evolutionists generally side with atheistic evolution teaching that mankind slowly evolved from primitive life forms by means of animal evolutionary stages through long ages. They teach that a race of subhuman men lived thousands of years before Adam was born. God then selected Adam from among this race, breathed the breath of God into him, and thus, rendered him no longer an animal but a man. Then God placed Adam in the Garden of Eden. Hence, Adam was spiritually, but not physically, the first member of the new human race.

Scientist R. J. Berry, one of the most vocal spokesmen for theistic evolution, writes:

A Christian need have no problem with fossil man and his discussions of the relationship of modern man with other hominoids, because he is told God created . . . man in existing material. There is certainly no difficulty in believing God could have carried out this special creation in a hominoid ape. There is no reason to believe the hominoid would change morphologically or genetically in any way that would be detectable to an anthropologist (R. J. Berry, *Creation and Evolution,* edited by Derek Burke, Leicester, England, Inter-Varsity Press: 1985, p. 80).

According to this view, when God put His spirit in Adam and he became a life-giving soul, a new relationship developed spiritually, not physically. Theologian John Stott adds:

It seems perfectly possible to reconcile the historicity of Adam with at least some (theistic) evolutionary theory.

Many biblical Christians in fact do so, believing them to be not entirely incompatible. To assert the historicity of an original pair who sinned through disobedience is one thing; it is quite another to deny all evolution and to assert that separate and special creation of everything both subhuman creatures and Adam's body. The suggestion (for it is no more than this) does not seem to be against Scripture and therefore impossible that when God made man in His own image, what He did was to stamp His own likeness on one of the many 'hominoids' which appear to have been living at the time (John Stott, The Church of England Newspaper, June 7, 1968).

Adam's Sin

R. J. Berry says the fall did not cause sin and death to enter into the world:

The fall did not lead to physical death . . . and we are wrong to infer that disease and suffering are necessarily and directly a result of sin—Christ Himself pointed out that this was a misreading of Scripture (Lk. 13:1-4). Biological Adam can be studied by anthropologists and evolutionists; spiritually—that is truly human—Adam can be understood and studied only by believers (Heb. 11:3) (R. J. Berry, *Creation and Evolution*, p. 105).

Scientist Tim Hawthorne writes:

If Adam and Eve were immortal, the mind boggles at the consequences of the instruction 'Be fruitful and increase your number' (Genesis 1:23)—an earth soon over-populated with immortal descendants! . . . The world of Genesis which God called good must have included pain and death if the living creatures described were anything like those we know today (Tim Hawthorne, *Windows on Science and Faith*, Inter-Varsity Press, Leicester, England: 1986, p. 88).

Language Of Genesis

Theistic evolutionists do not hold to a literal reading of the text of Genesis. They believe that Genesis is allegory, poetry or saga. Scientists Walter Hearne and Richard Hendry wrote:

The authors of this chapter consider the expressions of Scripture regarding the creation of life to be sufficiently figurative to imply little or no limitations on possible mechanisms (Walter Hearne and Richard Hendry, "The Origin of Life," *Evolution and Christian Thought Today*, Russell L. Mixter, editor, Grand Rapids: Eerdmans, 1959, p. 69).

Two other writers conclude:

It is mistaken to treat the first chapter of Genesis as science. It is a literary statement of the universal Lordship of God, and mankind's utter dependence upon him. It is a story of the wonder of our creation, yet the awfulness of our rebellion . . . .

Genesis then rings as true as ever, whether one follows an evolutionary account of biological origins or not (Vernon Blackmore and Andrew Page, *Evolution: The Great Debate*, Oxford, England: Lion Publishing, 1989, p. 188,189).

Jesus' Testimony

Theistic Evolutionists do not regard Jesus' testimony to Genesis as solving the matter of interpretation. Hawthorne writes:

Now Jesus certainly accepted the Genesis account as authoritative, for instance when he referred to God's making male and female humans in discussing divorce. But to argue that taking it as authoritative means he was endorsing a particular literalistic interpretation is to beg the question. The argument assumes that the early chapters of Genesis were written as a plain factual narrative. Many reverent students of the Old Testament will disagree (Tim Hawthorne, *Windows on Science and Faith*, p. 26).

R. J. Berry considers Jesus comments on Genesis as being irrelevant. He dismisses Jesus' statement in Matthew 19:4 and Peter's statement concerning creation in 2 Peter 3:5 by saying, "The ... two passages are not relevant and it is not clear they imply a literal reading" (R. J. Berry, *Creation and Evolution*, p. 56).

Results Of Science

Theistic evolutionists consider that modern science has proven evolution to be true therefore they feel the need to make the Scripture teach it. R. J. Berry cites non-Christian scientist Richard Lewontin who emphatically states that evolution is a fact:

It is time for students of the evolutionary process, especially those who have been misquoted and used by creationists, to state clearly that evolution is *fact*, not theory, and that what is at issue within biology are questions of detail of the process and the relative importance of different mechanisms of evolution (R. C. Lewontin, cited by R. J. Berry, *Creation and Evolution*, p. 105).

No Conflict?

Some non-Christians, such as Steve Allen, see no conflict between accepting evolution and believing in the existence of God:

Although it is absurd for literalist fundamentalists to deny the existence of evolution, given that the reality of that process is readily observable, it is equally erroneous to suggest that if evolution has occurred, the mere fact of its existence disproves the possibility that there is a God. In reality, there is no necessary connection or lack of connection between evolution and God. The majority of well-educated Christians and members of other religions believe, in fact, that evolution has simply been God's practical method of creating and developing all aspects of nature that are alive, which is to say plants and animals. It is apparently only fundamentalists who are confused about this (Steve Allen, *Steve Allen on Religion, The Bible, and Morality,* Buffalo, New York: Prometheus Books, 1990, p. 94).

Summary

We can summarize theistic evolution as follows: The first three chapters of Genesis are a mix of history and allegory. Theistic evolution cannot take the creation narrative literally. The theistic evolutionist assumes that all forms of life evolved along evolutionary lines. However, these humanlike creatures lacked the ability to communicate with God. So God selected one chosen pair from the species and provided that which was missing—a spirit. After they failed to obey His commandments God banished them from His presence and sentenced them to spiritual death. This punishment was handed down to all their descendants making the Christ's death on the cross necessary to atone for our sins.

At first glance, this approach accepts the Bible as inspired and authoritative, Adam and Eve as historical persons, as well as Darwinian evolution. Hence, the integrity of the Scripture is maintained, as well as acceptance of the "fact" of evolution.

These points are generally made in the case for theistic evolution. Those who hold to theistic evolution resent the implication that they are siding with evolutionists against creation. The claim to believe both. Evolution, they believe, is the mechanism God used. They say they are not debating against creation but rather against a non-evolutionary interpretation of it. The issue is not can a Bible believing Christian accept theistic evolution? It is obvious they can. The real question is *should* a Bible-believing Christian endorse this theory?

20

CAN THEISTIC EVOLUTION SOLVE THE CONTROVERSY BETWEEN CREATION AND EVOLUTION?

Is it possible that theistic evolution can solve the controversy between special creation and the theory of atheistic evolution? The answer is no. Theistic evolution does not fit the biblical account for a great number of reasons. The following are only a few of the problems that result in holding to a belief in theistic evolution.

Forced Interpretation

To begin with, the idea of theistic evolution does not result from a normal reading of the Bible. It is a forced interpretation of the text that does not accept the straightforward literal meaning. Theistic evolution reinterprets the clear statements of Scripture, attempting to make the Bible fit the modern theory of evolution. For this reason alone, it is suspect. Paul Zimmerman writes:

> In asking whether or not theistic evolution may be found in the text, we must come to grips with the question as to what kind of literature we have in Genesis 1. Unless we decide the kind of literature we are dealing with, we

cannot perform good exegesis. If it is historical prose, that is one thing. If it is poetry or myth or saga or symphony, that is quite another (Paul A. Zimmerman, "The Word of God Today", *Creation, Evolution, and God's Word*, Paul A. Zimmerman, editor, St. Louis: Concordia Publishing House, 1972, p. 102).

The Scriptures, from the first page to the last, treat the creation account in Genesis as having actually occurred. Nowhere is there a hint that it is myth or allegory. We should treat this account the same way as the biblical writers.

Evolution Is Atheism

As we have mentioned earlier, evolution, when taken to its logical end, equals atheism. Prominent humanist, Sir Julian Huxley has stated:

Darwinism removed the whole idea of God as the creator of organisms from the sphere of rational discussion. I think we can dismiss entirely all idea of a supernatural overriding mind being responsible for the evolutionary process (Sir Julian Huxley, *Issues in Evolution*, Sol Tax, editor, Chicago: University of Chicago Press, 1960, p. 45).

The *Encyclopaedia Brittanica* wrote of evolution.

Darwin did two things: he showed that evolution was a fact contradicting scriptural legends of creation and that its cause, natural selection, was automatic with no room for divine guidance or design (Encyclopaedia Brittanica, *Macropaedia*, Volume 7, 1979, p. 23).

Nigel Cameron writes:

One of the greatest of Christian thinkers, Professor Charles Hodge of Princeton, wrote a short book at the height of the controversy over Darwin, in the title of which he asked the question: What is Darwinism? The answer that he gave is also the answer I should give. In its assumptions, and in its implications, it is atheism (Nigel

Cameron, *Evolution and the Authority of The Bible,* Exeter, England: Paternoster Press, 1983, p. 10).

Darwin recognized the implications of his theory. To attempt to wed them together fits neither because it does injustice to what both are attempting to say.

Creator Versus Natural Processes

The heart of the theory of evolution explains all of reality apart from a Creator. Natural and random forces are the only things at work. Design and purpose are not in their vocabulary. The theory of evolution explains everything by a purely natural process; there is no need for God. Thus, at its basic intent, the theory of evolution is at odds with the Bible.

Finished Or Unfinished?

The Book of Genesis speaks of a finished creation:

Thus the heavens and the earth, and all the host of them were finished (Genesis 2:1).

The Bible says that after God had finished creating He rested. Malachi 2:10 reads, "Had not God created us?" Creation of mankind is viewed in Scripture as a historical event that is now past.

Evolution, on the other hand, is an unfinished process. How is it that one may believe both? Either God finished creating, as Genesis states, or natural processes that began millions of years in history past are still going on.

The Bible says, "For in six days God created the earth." In the Old Testament, every Sabbath Day, the Israelites recognized the fact that God created the universe. Theistic evolution has nothing from which to rest. What could be the meaning of rest for God who allowed evolutionary processes to go on for billions of years? There is nothing completed to rest from, no perfection to celebrate. Theistic evolution has no room for a God who rests. Every weekday should remind us that God created the earth in separate steps and every seventh day testifies that God wants us to remember it.

Furthermore, if nothing ceased on the seventh day then Genesis 2:1-3 is either meaningless or a lie. The clear meaning of the seventh day is that God completed a series of creative acts and thereafter deals with the universe in a fundamentally different manner. He is now working through natural processes guided by providence.

Evolution, by contrast, is an ongoing process which has continued from the beginning of the universe to this day. The theistic evolutionist must remove Genesis 2:1-3 out of his Bible, since for him nothing has ceased. There is no seventh day, or day of rest within the evolution model.

Logical Conclusion

Theistic evolution must be taken to its logical conclusion. Curtly F. Mather writes:

> When a theologian accepts evolution as the process used by the creator, he must be willing to go all the way with it. Not only is it an orderly process, it is a continuing one. Nothing was finished on any seventh day: the process of creation is still going on. The golden age for man—if any—is in the future, not in the past . . . Moreover the creative processes of evolution is not to be interrupted by any supernatural intervention . . . The spiritual aspects of the life of man are just as surely a product of the processes called evolution as are his brain and nervous system (C.F. Mather, *Science Ponders Religion*, Harlow Shapley, editor, New York: Appleton Century Croft, Inc., 1960, pp. 37,38).

Adam's Creation

Theistic evolution contradicts what the Bible says happened about the creation of Adam. The idea that God took a subhuman and developed him into a man is not taught in Scripture. The Bible says:

> And the Lord God formed man of the dust of the ground, and breathed into his nostrils the breath of life; and man became a living being (Genesis 2:7).

Notice the progression: God formed man out of the dust of the ground, breathed His spirit into man's nostrils, then man became a living soul. The Bible clearly says that man was created by God from the dust of the earth. "Dust" does not mean a subhuman creature. After Adam had sinned, God said to him:

> In the sweat of your face you shall eat bread till you return to the ground, for out of it you were taken; for dust you are, and to dust you shall return (Genesis 3:19).

Upon his death Adam was to return to dust, not to an animal body!

Scripture also emphasizes that mankind was created male and female in the image of God:

> Then God said, 'Let Us make man in Our image, according to Our likeness' . . . So God created man in His own image; in the image of God He created him; male and female He created them (Genesis 1:26,27).

Immediately upon creation, Adam was fully man. There was no intermediate half-man/half-ape before his creation. Special creation says Adam became a living soul in an act of creation, while theistic evolution says man inherits life from an animal.

New Testament

The New Testament assumes a literal creation of Adam. Adam is a type of Christ who is to come:

> Nevertheless death reigned from Adam to Moses, even over those who had not sinned according to the likeness of the transgression of Adam, who is a type of Him who was to come (Romans 5:14).

The first Adam became a living being:

> And so it is written, 'The first man Adam became a living being.' The last Adam a life-giving spirit (1 Corinthians 15:45).

For Adam was first formed then Eve (1 Timothy 2:13).

Adam was made from the dust of the earth while Eve was made from the side of Adam. Therefore, Paul can say:

And He has made us one blood every nation of men to dwell on all the face of the earth (Acts 17:26).

In First Corinthians 15, the Apostle Paul discussed the literal bodily resurrection of Christ and of believers. He wrote:

For as in Adam all die, so also in Christ shall all be made alive (1 Corinthians 15:22).

From the construction 'For as . . . so also' it is clear that if all do not die in Adam, then none shall be made alive in Christ. If Adam is not a literal historical person, then the Christian has no hope of the resurrection. If Adam is merely figurative, then our resurrection is merely figurative. Elsewhere, Paul not only confirms the Genesis account, he relates it to Jesus:

For it is the God who commanded light to shine out of darkness who has shone in our hearts to give the light of the knowledge of the glory of God in the face of Jesus Christ (2 Corinthians 4:6).

Creation Of Eve

The Bible says Eve, the first woman, was created by a supernatural direct act of God. She was made from Adam's side. The biblical account of the creation of Eve is rejected by theistic evolutionists. They say man and woman evolved together from some ape-like creature over a span of several million years. However, the writers of the New Testament support the literal truth of this account of Eve's creation:

For man is not from woman, but woman from man (1 Corinthians 11:8).

Eve is called the mother of all the living (Genesis 3:20). This also contradicts theistic evolution. Theistic evolution teaches that the woman came from a female animal not a human male (Adam) as the Scriptures teach.

Distinction Between Man and Animals

The Bible also makes the distinction between man and animals:

All flesh is not the same flesh, but there is one kind of flesh of men, another flesh of beasts (1 Corinthians 15:39).

Man, according to Scripture, has been made in the image of God, and is distinct from the rest of creation. Theistic evolution basically teaches that all flesh is one flesh. All of creation—man, animals and plants—are related according to the evolutionary model. The theory of theistic evolution strips away the dignity of man made in the image of God.

Redefined Good

After each creative act God gives us a status report: it was very good. When God finished His creation He pronounced it as very good (Genesis 1:31). Yet if one accepts theistic evolution, then the idea of good will have to be redefined. Evolutionary theory teaches the struggle for existence, survival of the fittest, the elimination of the weak, and death. If God permitted this method to occur for millions of years to bring life to its present state would He have pronounced creation good? The answer is no. To assert that God would have said everything was good after having been brought about by millions of years of death, struggle, and dying is inconsistent with the character of the God of the Bible.

Death

Theistic evolution denies that death resulted from sin. If man descended from lower forms of life, then death had already been in existence. If Adam were merely a male ape in whom God put His Spirit, then his body would have been subject to death and disease as other apes. Evolution says that death existed millions of years before man appeared.

Thus, sin would not have been the cause for his death. But the Bible says it was:

Therefore, just as through one man sin entered the world, and death through sin, and thus death spread to all men (Romans 5:12).

Theistic evolution not only disregards the literal interpretation of the Bible, it also contradicts what the Bible says. The Scripture says that death is not something that is natural for mankind. It is an enemy, the result of man's fall:

The sting of death is sin (1 Corinthians 15:56).

Death is a painful reminder of our sin. How can death be reconciled in a world that is very good? Death, however, is essential for the theory of evolution.

Not God's Means

The theory of evolution stands against the scientific evidence. On a scientific level evolution could not be God's means of creation. The evolutionary processes, mutation and selection do not create. They only vary and preserve traits that already exist. They are effective only after creation has already taken place. Duane Gish writes:

According to the theory of evolution, ultimately all of evolution is due to mutations. No-one can rationally deny that mutations are random events. In fact, it is fair to say, (and most evolutionist do say) that mutations are mistakes. They are equivalent to typographical errors. Further, no rational scientist would deny that practically all mutations are harmful (in fact, it is difficult if not impossible to prove that any are beneficial). Many are indeed lethal.

Furthermore, the evolutionary process has apparently lead to many dead ends. Evolution would certainly constitute the most wasteful, inefficient, cruel method God could have used to create. The concept of evolution is thus totally inconsistent with the attributes of God as revealed in Scripture (Duane Gish, *Creation and Evolution*, Derek Burke, editor, Leicester, England: Inter-Varsity Press, 1985, pp. 140,141).

Scientist Henry Morris observes:

Surely an omniscient God could devise a better process of creation than the random, wasteful, inefficient trial and error charade of the so-called geological ages, and certainly a loving, merciful God would never be guilty of a creative process that would involve the suffering and death of multitudes of innocent animals, in the process of arriving at man millions of years later.

It should be obvious that the God of the Bible would create everything complete and good, right from the start. In fact, He testified that all of it was "very good" (Genesis 1:31). The wastefulness and randomness and cruelty which is now so evident in the world (both the groaning creation of the present and in the fossilized world of the past) must represent an intrusion into His creation, not a mechanism for its accomplishment. God would never do a thing like that, except in judgment in sin! (Henry Morris, *Creation and the Modern Christian*, El Cajon, California: Master Book Publishers, 1985, p. 42).

Limited Variation

The theory of evolution teaches that man developed from a common ancestor with the ape. According to the theory of evolution, animals have also developed along this line. The Bible, however, does not allow for this:

Then God said, 'Let the earth bring forth the living creature according to its kind: cattle and creeping thing and beast of the earth, each according to its kind'; and it was so (Genesis 1:24).

As we have already mentioned, the Bible teaches that there are definite limits, or fixed boundaries to the variations that can occur. This means that pigs produce pigs, dogs produce dogs, etc. There is no crossing of these kinds to produce some bizarre creature.

Upward Or Downward?

The theory of evolution teaches that man and the universe are continuing on an upward development. The Bible teaches that everything was perfect in the beginning and that the effect of sin is that man and the universe are on a downward trend:

> For creation was subjected to futility, not willingly, but because of Him who subjected it in hope; because the creation itself also will be delivered from the bondage of corruption into the glorious liberty of the children of God (Romans 8:20,21).

After Adam and Eve sinned God pronounced judgment upon them and upon the earth:

> To the woman He said: 'I will greatly multiply your sorrow and your conception; in pain you shall bring forth children; your desire shall be for your husband, and he shall rule over you.' Then to Adam He said, ' . . . Cursed is the ground for your sake; in toil you shall eat of it all the days of your life. Both thorns and thistles it shall bring forth for you . . . In the sweat of your face you shall eat bread till you return to the ground (Genesis 3:16-19).

The earth, as well as humanity, was to suffer the consequences of sin. Nature was created perfect but was corrupted when Adam disobeyed God. Evolution teaches that nature is growing better by change.

Different Order

There is a different order of things between the Bible and the theory of evolution:

Bible: First life was land plants (Genesis 1:11).
Evolution: Marine organisms evolved first.

Bible: Fruit trees before fish (Genesis 1:11,20,21).
Evolution: Fish before fruit trees.

Bible: Birds before insects (Genesis 1:20-31).
Evolution: Insects before birds.

Bible: Whales before reptiles (Genesis 1:20-31).
Evolution: Reptiles before whales.

Bible: Man before rain (Genesis 2:5).
Evolution: Rain before man.

Other Differences

Apart from the different order of things there are other differences between the Bible and the theory of evolution.

The Bible says birds and fish were created on the fifth day (Genesis 1:20,21), but the theory of evolution says that fish evolved hundreds of millions of years before birds appeared.

The Bible says the different varieties of marine life were created all at once (Genesis 1:20-21), while evolution states that marine life gradually evolved from a primitive single cell.

All Of Scripture

One of the issues rarely dealt with by theistic evolutionists concerns the entire teaching of Scripture. They emphasize that Genesis is to be understood poetically or as an allegory, yet the biblical account of creation is found in both testaments. Furthermore, essential doctrines of the Christian faith are built on the idea of a literal understanding of the account.

Experts Divided

The perception is often given that all scientists accept evolution, but this is not the case. The experts are divided. Though a majority of scientists believe in evolution, there are notable scientists who either do not believe it or who believe that it is a bad theory.

Which God?

If a person says they believe in God and evolution the question arises, "What God are you talking about?" It is certainly not the God of the Bible. He is not the God who created all things by the Word of His power, or the One described in the book of Psalms, who holds the breath of every living thing by the Word of His power. He is not the God described in the book of Psalms, who controls life and death, seed-time and harvest, wind and rain. Those who accept evolution are left with a God who started the world on its way but then left it to struggle painfully upwards toward it knows not what. What a contrast to the God described in the Bible who orders all things in nature and among men after the counsel and purpose of His own will. David Rosevear comments:

> But can we have our cake and eat it? Can we believe in a God who used evolution to bring about his plan? What kind of god would this be?
> —He would be a god who does not say what he means or means what he says. The order of creation in Genesis is all wrong and the time scale is preposterous. He said he made plants according to their kind, with their seed within themselves to reproduce according to their kind. He said he made animals according to their kind also. If God used evolution, this account in Genesis is plain wrong.
> —He is a god who uses death, struggle and chance to achieve his purposes—a cruel and gambling god (David Rosevear, *Creation Science*, Chichester, England: New Wine Press, 1991, p. 20).

Which Part Do We Believe?

Accepting theistic evolution means some parts of the Bible are true—while other parts are false. How do we decide what parts to believe and which parts not to? Is the Bible true when it tells us that Jesus Christ was God in human form but false when it says, "All things were made by Him?" Do we believe the story of Abraham in the book of Genesis but reject the story of creation in the same book? Can we believe anything the

Bible teaches about God if we accept that some parts of Scripture are myths?

Testimony Of Jesus

Jesus testified that Adam and Eve were created by God:

Have you not read that He who made them at the beginning made them male and female? (Matthew 19:4).

Jesus said God "made" Adam and Eve. He does not teach that some subhuman creature had a spirit breathed into him and thus became "Adam." If Adam and Eve were subhuman animals before receiving God's Spirit they would already have been male and female. This would contradict the statements in Genesis 1:27 and the words of Jesus in Matthew 19:4.

Jesus also confirmed they were made as *adult* male and female, ready for marriage.

Confirmed Genesis

Jesus certifies as accurate the very language of Genesis. This sets His authority against those who would read another account of Genesis. Jesus said, Adam was made man in the beginning. When Jesus spoke of Adam and Eve being "made," He used the aorist tense of the Greek verb. This tense stressed the fact that the pair was made by single acts of creation. Had Jesus believed that the Adam and Eve were a product of vast ages of time, he would have employed the Greek imperfect tense, which emphasizes progressive action at some time in the past. Thus, the Lord actually verbally refuted the concept of evolutionary development, and He was in a position to know what occurred at the beginning, since the Bible says He was there (John 1:1), and was *the* active agent of creation (Colossians 1:16).

Unresolved Questions

There are other questions for which theistic evolution has no answers. If people die because of sin, were pre-Adamites immortal? Did Adam's contemporaries die when he sinned? Scripture says that man's sin was the cause of death:

> Therefore, just as through one man sin entered the world, and death through sin, and thus death spread to to all men, because all sinned (Romans 5:12).

The theory of theistic evolution leaves so many questions unanswered.

Summary

The problems with theistic evolution can be summarized as follows:

1. Forced Interpretation

It is not possible to reconcile the theory of evolution with a normal interpretation of the Bible. To hold to theistic evolution, one must interpret Genesis as poetry or allegory.

2. Finished Or Unfinished Process

Creation is a finished process. God has ceased creating and now He is preserving His creation. Evolution is an ongoing process that is still occurring.

3. Creator Or Natural Process

The Bible teaches that a Creator was intimately involved in the process of creation, while theistic evolution leaves things to natural processes.

4. Limited Or Unlimited Variation

Evolution teaches an unlimited variation between life forms, while the Bible makes it clear there is a limit to variation.

5.   Upward Or Downward Trend

Evolution teaches things are progressing to the better while the Bible teaches man has fallen from His perfect state.

6.   Different Order Of Events

The creation account in Genesis and the theory of evolution have a different order of events. Though theistic evolution wants to have the best of both worlds, the difficulties between evolution and special creation are ignored or glossed over.

7.   Extinct Organisms Before Men

Man, according to evolution, came late onto the scene of life forms, with animals being extinct before his coming. The Bible says Adam was to have dominion over *all* the created forms.

8.   Death Before Sin

The Bible says sin was the cause of death. Theistic evolution believes and teaches that death was in the world prior to sin.

9.   Distinction Between Man And Animals

The Bible makes the distinction between man and animals, while theistic evolution assumes only a spiritual distinction.

10.   Redefined Good

Theistic evolution has to redefine God's creation as good because it believes there was death and sin before Adam's fall.

11.   Not God's Means

Evolution is a very inefficient way of bringing about new species. The whole idea of chance evolution goes against the character of God.

12. Man: Image Of God, Not Ape

Man is a special creation according to Scripture, not merely a trousered ape.

13. Creation Of Eve

Theistic evolution contradicts the Bible concerning the creation of Eve. Her supernatural creation refutes any idea of theistic evolution.

14. Which God?

The God of the Bible is not the same God in which the evolutionists believe. Theistic evolution reduces the role of God as Creator and makes Him more a spectator who supervises the ongoing process.

15. Testimony Of Jesus

The testimony of Jesus contradicts the idea of theistic evolution. He believed in a literal creation of Adam and Eve.

16. Evolutionists Reject The Compromise

The majority of evolutionists either ignore theistic evolution or laugh at it. They will have nothing to do with this theory.

Conclusion

It is theoretically possible that God could use the evolutionary process to "create" the world. It is hypothetically as possible as "special creation." However, this is not the issue. We are not engaging in speculative discussion or debating what God *might* do. Rather, we are discussing what God has done. There is a world of difference between the two. For the Christian, we must consider the question in the light of Scripture. We must find out what the Bible says God did.

21

WHY DO SOME CHRISTIANS BELIEVE IN EVOLUTION?

As we have seen, a study of Scripture shows that God did not employ the mindless, chance methods of Darwinian evolution. This being the case, why do so many Christians believe in some form of evolution? There are a number of reasons as to why this is so.

Lack Of Knowledge

First, many people lack knowledge of what the Bible says about the subject. They are unaware that the Bible and evolution are not compatible. They suppose that theistic evolution is a philosophy acceptable to the Christian faith, not having contemplated the contradictions involved. They have not yet encountered or fully considered the Bible's teaching on this subject.

Reinterpret Scripture

Some people attempt to make the Bible fit the evidence. A person may feel the need to reinterpret the Bible to fit the so-called assured results of contemporary evolutionary science. Albert Pieters wrote:

If a Christian believer is inclined to yield as far as possible to the theory of organic evolution, he can hold that man's body was prepared by God through such a natural process, and that when this process had reached a certain stage, God took one of the man-like brutes so produced, and made him the first human being, by endowing him with a human soul and a morally responsible nature . . . In such a conception there is nothing contrary to the Bible (Albert Pieters, *Notes on Genesis*, Grand Rapids: William B. Eerdmans, 1943, p. 45).

Theologian R. Laird Harris offers an appropriate comment:

I am appalled at the freedom with which our Christian scientists are toying with the Biblical texts. I may soften that by adding that our theologians are doing so too and so the scientists naturally are taking it up. But the scientists should have a chance to hear the criticisms of various theologians rather than jumping to the first far out exegesis of Genesis that seems to meet the scientific need (R. Laird Harris, "Letter to the Editor," *Journal of American Scientific Affiliation*, December 16, 1964, p. 127).

Overestimate Evidence

Scientists, Christian and non-Christian alike, can easily overestimate the supposed evidences of evolution outside of their particular field. A paleontologist, for example, may be persuaded that modern biology has genuine proof of the theory of evolution. As a scientist he respects the reports of other scientists, even though the evidence in his particular field may be lacking. This being the case, a Christian scientist could advocate the idea that God did create the universe in the beginning but allowed things to develop through gradual natural processes. Consequently, he keeps his Christian faith and also keeps in line with present-day scientific theory.

Convinced It Is True

A final reason that many Christians believe in evolution is that they sincerely believe that it is the correct answer to the question of origins. Having examined the evidence, they conclude that the theory of evolution best fits the facts.

These are some, but by no means all, of the reasons why some people hold to the theory of theistic evolution. However, as we have seen, both the scriptural and scientific evidence do not encourage one to accept this position.

Does It Matter?

It is important to keep this issue in perspective. Creationism is not the gospel, though some treat it as such. A person can be a Christian and still hold to theistic evolution. However, one who holds such a viewpoint is not being consistent with what the Bible teaches. The theistic evolutionist has to assume much of the Bible is meant to be read poetically or allegorically. J. H. Newman wrote:

> When I show a man he is inconsistent, I make him decide whether of the two he loves better, the portion of truth he already holds, or the portion of error.

We conclude, then, that theistic evolution is not a consistent position for a Christian to hold.

22

IS THERE A DIFFERENCE BETWEEN OURSELVES AND ANIMALS?

As we close our section on the creation/evolution controversy we focus on ourselves. What are human beings? Are we different from animals? Mark Twain said, "Man is the only animal that blushes—and the only animal that needs to!" Professor C.E.M. Joad noted that man is nothing but:

Fat enough for seven bars of soap; Iron enough for one medium-sized nail; Sugar enough for seven cups of tea; Lime enough to whitewash one chicken coop; Phosphorus enough to tip two thousand two hundred matches; Magnesium enough for one dose of salts; Potash enough to explode one toy crane; sulphur enough to rid one dog of fleas.

The Bible makes a clear distinction between man and animals:

All flesh is not the same flesh, but there is one kind of flesh of men, another flesh of beasts, another of fish, another of birds (1 Corinthians 15:39).

Man is different from all other animals in a number of ways:

1. Analytical Thought

Man can think analytically. He can analyze problems and come up with creative solutions. He is able to reason and philosophize about life. The reasoning powers in animals are limited.

2. True Language

Only man possesses true language and conceptual thought. He can communicate by using abstract symbols. The Bible says one of the first responsibilities given Adam by God was to name the animals (Genesis 2:19-23). Animals have no such capacities.

3. Recorded History

Another difference is that man can record and determine history. From the beginning of time, man has recorded his deeds for the benefit of future generations. There is no example of any animal recording their deeds for posterity.

4. Economics

Man is an economic being, able to transact complicated business and to administer goods and services under his control. God instructed Adam and Eve to take control of the earth and "subdue" it (Genesis 1:28). Animals do not transact business between each other.

5. Art

Man is an aesthetic being, capable of perceiving and appreciating beauty and intangible values. When animals build things, the process and resulting object serve a functional purpose. Animals do not create objects for the purpose of appreciation.

6. Morality

Man is an ethical being. He can distinguish between right and wrong. He can and does make moral judgments. He has a conscience. Only to man could God speak of "good" and "evil." Because of man's sense of justice and his ethical orientation, God could fairly punish him for his willful disobedience in the Garden of Eden.

7. Worship

Only man can experience faith. Man alone of all earthly creation can worship his Creator. He alone can put his trust in the guidance and leadership of God.

8. Bury Its Dead

Man is the only living creature that buries its dead. There is no example of animals doing any type of ceremonial burial as does man.

The above list, though not exhaustive, points out that there are many things that separate man from animals. We could also add such things as: creativity, invention, imagination, abstract reasoning, love (at various levels), a will, and a conscience.

Human Life Is Different

It is important to note the significant difference between humans and other life forms. Not only are humans different from plants, but humans are also different from animals. Only humans, according to the Bible, are made in "God's image." Only humans possess the will and self-consciousness that distinguish us so sharply from even the most "advanced" and intelligent animals. Anatomist Kingsley Mortimer discusses that difference:

To the scientist, man is an animal, graciously self-designated as *homo sapiens* . . . If he is, at least, he is still the only one discussing what kind of animal he is. Few, however, would deny that man, animal or not has features without parallel in any other member of that kingdom. We are quite familiar with the physical evidence that marks out homo sapiens—the erect posture, the grasping thumb, the cerebral hemispheres. These are all acceptable criteria and have been with us for a long time. Few men take pride in them, but rather take them for granted . . . standard equipment. What puts man in the luxury class among all forms of life is his unique capacity for thought, and his possession of free will. He can do as he likes; he can go it alone. By his own choice, he can know the mystery of loneliness and solitary rebellion. Indeed, the very capacity to be rebellious or miserable is the property of man alone. For who ever hears of a miserable rose or a rebellious kangaroo? (Kingsley Mortimer, "An Anatomist's Testimony,"*Why I Am Still a Christian*, E. M. Blaiklock, editor, Grand Rapids, MI: Zondervan, pp. 138,139).

From the Bible, as well as from observing both man and animals, it can be seen that there is a vast difference between the two. Francis Schaeffer comments:

Secular history can tell us much about our past as a human race, and therefore our own place in it. But no matter how much writing we turn up and translate, no matter how many excavations we make and how many artifacts we study, secular history has not unearthed a clue to help explain the final 'why' of what we find.

All the way back to the dawn of our studies we find man still being man. Wherever we turn—to the caves in the Pyrenees, to the Sumerians, and further back to the Neanderthaler man burying his dead with flower petals— it makes no difference: Everywhere men show by their art and their acts that they observed themselves to be unique. And they are unique, unique as men in the midst of non-men (Francis Schaeffer, *Genesis in Space and Time*, Downers Grove, Illinois: InterVarsity Press, 1972, pp. 158,159).

Man—Made In God's Image

The Bible says man has been made in the image and likeness of God. Man was the climax of God's creation, having been created on the sixth day. Though last in order he is first in importance:

So God created man in His own image; in the the image of God He created him; male and female He created them (Genesis 1:27).

In the day that God created man. He made him in the likeness of God. He created them male and female, and blessed them and called them Mankind in the day they were created (Genesis 5:1,2).

What does it mean that man was created in God's image? To say that man was made in the image of God means that God and man have many things in common. When God created man He gave him such things as personality, choice, emotions, morality, and creativity.

Personality

Both man and God have personality, that is to say, they can both think and communicate as rational beings. They each have personal identity that is separate from other rational beings and from non-living things. Man and God also have the ability to communicate to other rational beings:

And have put on the new man who is renewed in knowledge according to the image of Him who created him (Colossians 3:10).

Choice

A second common trait between man and God is choice. Both God and man are beings who have the ability to choose, though God does not have the ability to choose evil. Neither God nor man is programmed or forced to make any choices. This freedom was given to man by God and man is responsible for the choices he makes.

Both man and God have emotions. For example, each can give love and receive love. God, as well as man, can be angry. Both man and God have the capacity to feel and express emotions.

Man and God both have a moral sense of right and wrong. Each knows and understands the difference between good and evil. The Bible says:

> And that you put on the new man which was created according to God, in righteousness and true holiness (Ephesians 4:24).

Another attribute that God and man have in common is creativity. The Bible says God created the universe and everything within it. Man also is a creative being, having been given this ability by God.

Summary

Man is different from the animals. Both biblical and scientific evidence demonstrate this. Man alone has the capacity to know and worship God because he has been made in God's image after God's likeness.

Summary To Section Three

As we have looked at the biblical account of creation and the evidence to support it, we find there are excellent reasons for believing it to be true. There are no logical arguments for disbelieving in the Genesis account of creation and accepting the theory of mindless evolution.

Centered Around Jesus

For the Christian, the creation/evolution debate must be seen in the context of the person of Jesus Christ. It is possible for a person to prefer a creationist model of origins over an evolutionary model and still not be a Christian. While arguments can be given to show that a "creator" best fits the evidence of the universe around us, we need the Bible to inform us who this Creator is. Scientific creationism, apart from the Bible, cannot lead us to the knowledge of the true and living God. Award-winning scientist E. H. Andrews provides a helpful illustration of this point:

> Hoyle and Wickramasinghe in their book *Evolution from Space* . . . come to the conclusion that life could not have evolved without the intervention of intelligent beings. But they are at pains to point out that these 'gods' are not to be confused with the God of the Bible or indeed the gods of any traditional religion. They remain blind, therefore to the true being and nature of God, in spite of their creationist insights. It is in Christ, and in Christ alone, that the invisible God effectually reveals himself to man (E.H. Andrews, "Biblical Creation and Scientific Creationism—Is There a Conflict?", *Concepts in Creationism*, E. H. Andrews, W. Gitt, and W. J. Ouweneel, editors, Welwyn, Herts, England: Evangelical Press, 1986, p. 58).

Though the evidence for the creative design is clear for all mankind to see, Christians have to be careful in appealing to it alone to prove their case for creation. Again we quote award-winning scientist E. H. Andrews:

> When we say it is not possible to explain any particular phenomenon (such as the origin of life, for example) in terms of natural law, we are appealing to 'the God of the gaps'. We observe some symbiosis, or some wonder such as the migration of birds, and cannot conceive how an evolutionary account of origins could possibly expla , that which we observe. But the evolutionist always has the answer that next week, or next year, or in a hundred years' time, when science has progressed sufficiently, we shall be able to explain these things by natural law. All we are doing, says the evolutionist, is introducing ʹod when we run out of knowledge. It is very difficult to disagree with that argument as long as we stick to scientific reasoning, however convinced we may be that evolution is wrong and creation is right (E.H. Andrews, "Biblical Creation and Scientific Creationism—Is There a Conflict?", *Concepts in Creationism*, p. 50).

We again stress the need to place the issue of creation in an overall biblical context.

If the Bible is inspired by God, then its references to science and nature must be correct. But what about passages that are seemingly scientifically inaccurate? How are they to be explained?

In our next section we will examine certain passages in Scripture that are considered to be "scientific difficulties."

Scientific Difficulties
In Scripture

Where were you when I laid the foundations of the earth? Tell
Me if you have understanding. Who determined its
measurements? Surely you know! Or who stretched the line
upon it? To what were its foundations fastened? Or who
laid its cornerstone?
(Job 38:4-6)

23

DOES THE BIBLE MAKE
UNSCIENTIFIC STATEMENTS?

The Bible was written in what is termed the pre-scientific era, before the rise of modern science. Many books and articles have been written that accuse the Bible of giving scientifically inaccurate statements. Yet the Bible, if it is the Word of God, should be accurate when it touches upon the areas of science. Joseph Dillows writes:

It is obvious that the Bible is not a scientific textbook in the sense of giving detailed technical descriptions and mathematical formulations of natural phenomena. But this is not an adequate reason for questioning the objective accuracy of the numerous portions of Scripture which do deal with natural phenomena and historical events. The Bible is not a mathematic text either, but we expect that Daniel understands sixty-nine weeks by the phrase, "seven weeks and sixty-two weeks" (Dan 9:25). The Bible is not, strictly speaking, a historical textbook either, but we expect that when it alludes to things that can be historically verified, it should be accurate. Likewise, the Bible is not technically a textbook of modern science, but when it refers to things that can be measured or checked by modern science, it should be accurate (Joseph Dillow, *The Waters Above*, Chicago: Moody Press, 1981, p. 2).

Certain statements made in Scripture seem to be unscientific at first glance. A closer inspection of the evidence, however, will reveal that these supposed errors come from either a lack of understanding of what the Bible says or what science has proven. The following are some of the most often-raised scientific difficulties in the Bible.

Earth Center Of Solar System

One of the most common objections is that the Bible portrays the earth as the center of the solar system. Henry Morris writes:

This charge is most unjust since, we still use words and phrases of the same sort, simply because from our natural viewpoint the sun does rise in the morning, move across the sky and set in the evening. The whole science of nautical and engineering astronomy is based on the assumption, made purely for convenience, that the earth is the center of a great celestial sphere, moving along the surface of which in ordered paths are the sun, moon, planets, and stars. And as far as any practical usage is concerned, this is so. On this assumption, courses can be plotted, positions determined, and scores of other applications made (Henry Morris, *The Bible and Modern Science*, Chicago: Moody Press, 1968, pp. 6,7).

As we have mentioned, the biblical writers spoke of things as they appear from the vantage point of an observer. From that point of view the earth does revolve around the sun. There is an unfortunate tendency to accuse the Bible of being unscientific because it uses non-scientific language. How many of us hear our local television weather report state that "the rotation of the earth on its axis will move out of our area and out of direct sunlight at 6:30 this evening?" On the contrary, the common report is that "Sunset tonight will be at 6:30." The critic has a tendency to place greater restrictions on the language of the Bible than he does on himself and those around him. To do so is unfair and ultimately, unscientific.

However, there is another truth that the Scripture makes. The Bible makes it clear that the earth is the central heavenly body. This is not due to its position in space, but rather to its place in God's creative purpose. It is on this planet where God has chosen to work out His plan for time and eternity. Therefore, the earth does have a special place in the universe.

Primitive View Of The World

Another criticism leveled at Scripture is that it has a primitive view of the earth and the heavens. The Bible speaks of such things as the "four corners of the earth" and the earth "resting on pillars." These phrases supposedly show its unscientific character.

The Bible does speak of the four corners of the earth:

And will gather the dispersed of Judah from the four corners of the earth (Isaiah 11:12).

Does this teach that the earth is a quadrangle? Not at all. It is a figure of speech referring to the four points of the horizon. The same prophet in another place shows properly that the earth is round:

It is He who sits above the circle of the earth (Isaiah 40:22).

Scripture also says:

For the pillars of the earth are the Lord's (1 Samuel 2:8).

Does this mean that the biblical world view is that the earth is supported by pillars? Again, what we have here is a figurative statement. Elsewhere the Bible says the earth rests upon nothing:

He hangs the earth on nothing (Job 26:7).

Even today a better scientific description of the earth could not be given.

There are other statements of this sort that Scripture makes, many of them found in the book of Genesis. When examined closely they are not found to be unscientific (I have dealt with many of them in detail in my book, *Understanding the Early Chapters of Genesis*, Spokane, Washington: AusAmerica Publishers, 1993).

24

DOES THE HARE
CHEW ITS CUD?

One of the so-called scientific errors found in the Bible concerns the hare chewing its cud. It is a favorite illustration of unbelievers as to the "unscientific" nature of Scripture.

The Bible lists the hare as an unclean animal, one that is not fit for human consumption. The reason it gives is what has caused the controversy:

> The hare because it chews the cud but does not have cloven hooves, is unclean to you (Leviticus 11:6).

To be fit for human consumption the Bible said that an animal must chew its cud and divide the hoof. The hare is listed as an unclean animal because it does not have cloven hooves. However, the Scripture says that the hare chews its cud. There are those who accuse the Bible of being in error because the hare is not a ruminant, it does not chew its cud.

Appears To Chew

The solution to this question is that the hare gives the *appearance* of chewing the cud. In fact, Linnaeus at first classified the hare as a ruminant, even though the four-stomach apparatus was lacking. Moreover, the list of forbidden animals was intended to be a practical guide, not a scientific classification. When the Israelite went out in the wilds looking for food he might have concluded that these animals were fit to eat since they ruminated like the larger cattle and fed on the same kind of grass and herbs. This is why the law pointed out that they did not have hooves at all and therefore could not meet the requirements for edible flood. F. Duane Lindsay adds this comment:

> It is true that the coney and rabbit do not 'chew the cud' in the modern scientific sense, but their jaw movements and thoroughness in chewing fell within the empirical significance of the Hebrew phrase (F. Duane Lindsay,*The Bible Knowledge Commentary*, John Walvoord and Roy Zuck, eds., Wheaton, Illinois: Victor Books, 1985, pp. 190,191).

Therefore, the statement that the hare chews its cud should not be taken in the strict scientific classification. Moses listed things not as a comparative anatomist, but as things appeared to the observer.

25

DID THE SUN ACTUALLY STAND STILL IN JOSHUA'S LONG DAY?

Whenever the subject arises concerning biblical events and their relationship to science, the story of Joshua and the sun standing still is usually brought up. It is one of the favorite texts of unbelievers to demonstrate the ignorance of the writers of Scripture.

Sun Stood Still

In the tenth chapter of the Book of Joshua the following account is recorded:

Then Joshua spoke to the Lord in the day when the Lord delivered up the Amorites before the children of Israel, and he said in the sight of Israel: 'Sun, stand still over Gibeon; and Moon, in the Valley of Aijalon.' So the sun stood still, and the moon stopped, till the people had revenge upon their enemies. Is this not written in the book of Jasher? So the sun stood still in the midst of heaven, and did not hastened to go down for about a whole day. And there has been no day like that, before it or after it, that the Lord heeded a voice of a man; for the Lord fought for Israel (Joshua 10:12-14).

We know that the sun does not move around the earth causing day and night but rather the earth revolves around the sun. Why did Joshua address the sun rather than the earth? Did he believe the sun actually moved?

Language Of Appearance

As we have already mentioned, Scripture speaks in the language of appearance, the language of observation. From our point of view here on earth the sun does rise in the morning and set at night. From that vantage point Joshua addresses the sun with his request. Marten Woodstra, Old Testament authority, writes:

> The language that Joshua uses in addressing the sun and moon is the language of ordinary observation still used today in the scientific age. Probably Joshua and his contemporaries thought of the sun as moving around the earth, but his language should not be pressed to construct a "view of the universe" any more than should today's reference to the rising and setting of the sun (Marten Woodstra, *The Book of Joshua*, Grand Rapids, Eerdmans: 1981, p. 175).

Scientifically Accurate?

Some people feel that Joshua made a scientifically accurate request.

We might say, "How little Joshua knew." But he knew his God! He knew that God had promised to go before His people to fight their battles and give them victory (Joshua 10:8). And in this battle he saw victory in its grasp, but time was running out. If he didn't conquer the enemy before dark, they would regroup and attack Israel the next day. Knowing his God, his God's power, and his God's promise, he called out to God for help, and in the presence of all Israel, he commanded the "sun to stand still." But the sun was already standing still, Joshua. It is the earth that moves, not the sun. Why didn't Joshua cry out, "Earth quit moving," or "Earth, slow down your spinning on your axis to prolong time."

Joshua had no idea that his command slowed down 6.6 sextrillion tons of spinning gravel and water to give Israel victory over her enemies. But Joshua did know something that God had revealed to him. Over 3,000 years ago he said something that would have met the approval of today's scientific establishment. His command in the Hebrew language was not "Sun, stand thou still," but "Sun, cease acting, or "Sun, stop working." It was then that the gravitational pull of the sun affected the earth. It was then the earth began to slow down and the day was lengthened (Robert Boyd, *Boyd's Bible Handbook*, Eugene, Oregon: Harvest House, 1983 p. 124).

This argument is rather weak. It is not necessary to assume Joshua was scientifically sophisticated. It is more likely that God honored the spirit of his request than to assume Joshua had some scientific insight that was not shared by the people of his day.

Long Day Legends?

Some have argued that evidence for this long day is found in other cultures:

It is interesting to note that parallel accounts in the records of other nations show that the incident of "Joshua's Long Day" is not an isolated one. There is indisputable evidence from the modern science of ethnology that such an event occurred as Joshua records. In the ancient Chinese writings there is a legend of a long day. The Incas of Peru and the Aztecs of Mexico have a like record. There is a Babylonian and Persian legend of a day that was miraculously extended. Herodotus, an ancient historian, recounts that while in Egypt, priest showed him their temple records, and that he read of a day which was twice the natural length of any day that had ever been recorded (Robert Boyd, *Boyd's Bible Handbook*, pp. 122,123).

This, however, does not seem to be the case.

The record of the 'long day' has been much debated. Parallels have been found in Chinese, Egyptian and Mexican stories, but these will not coincide with the date or time of day (E.W. Maunder, JTVI, 1921, pp. 120-148); and an astronomical aberration would not have gone unrecorded in Babylon (John Lilley, *The New Layman's Bible Commentary*, G.C.D. Howley, F.F. Bruce, H.L. Ellison, eds., Grand Rapids, Michigan: Zondervan, 1979, pp. 320,321).

Many Questions

There are many questions that this account brings up. How are we to understand the phrase, "the sun stood still?" What was the nature of Joshua's command? Did he want more sunlight or less sunlight? Did he need more time to win the battle or did he need relief from the heat of the sun? If the earth actually stopped rotating for 24 hours would not incredible catastrophe occur to everything upon the planet?

Background

Before we examine the various views, it is important to know something of the background of the event. Joshua's army had marched all night from Gilgal to Gibeon, a distance of twenty miles, to do battle with their enemies.

Joshua needed the battle time prolonged because five strong kings had brought out their armies to fight his army in the open country. Joshua had the enemy on the run and he did not want them to get back to their fortified cities. More time was needed for his troops to catch them. To prevent their return more daylight was needed. Hence, he asked God to lengthen the day.

Sun Stopped

The text does say that the sun stopped. The Hebrew uses two words *daman* and *amad* which have the idea "to stop."

The word translated stand still (Heb *dom*) means literally to 'be silent' and frequently has the sense 'cease' or leave off' (cf. Ps. 35:15; La. 2:18). Similarly the word translated stayed (Heb *amad*), stood still in v. 13b, has the sense of 'cease' (cf. 2 Ki. 4:6; Jon. 1:15) (Hugh J. Blair, "Joshua," *The New Bible Commentary Revised*, D. Guthrie, J.A. Motyer, A.M. Stibbs, D.J. Wiseman eds., Leicester, England: Inter-Varsity Press, Third Edition, 1970, p. 244).

The fact that Joshua asked the sun to stop is not the issue. The question is, "In what sense did the sun stop?"

What Happened?

Joshua gave the command for the sun to "stand still." There have been a number of ways in which commentators have sought to understand what occurred:

1. The passage is poetical and not to be understood literally.

2. The sun "standing still" refers to an eclipse of the sun.

3. The earth actually stopped its rotation around the sun for almost twenty-four hours per Joshua's request.

4. The earth's rotation was slowed down, not stopped. This lengthened the day by almost twenty-four hours.

5. The sun and moon appeared to be out of their regular place by a supernaturally given mirage.

6. The sun stopped shining during the latter half of the day.

7. Rather than the day being prolonged, God prolonged the previous night.

We will look at each of these explanations and examine their strengths and weaknesses.

1.   Poetical

There are some Bible students who see this account as being a poetical description of the battle and not to be taken literally. Donald H. Madvig notes:

> The final statement in this verse [13] clearly favors the notion that the sun stood still or that it slowed down its course across the sky. In either event the problem for geophysics are so great that some other solution has been eagerly sought by scholars both liberal and conservative (Donald H. Madvig, "Joshua," *The Expositors Bible Commentary*, Frank E. Gaebelein, General editor, Grand Rapids: Zondervan, 1992, p. 303).

The *Pulpit Commentary* provides us with an example of interpreting the passage poetically:

> The poetic form of this passage is clear to anyone who has the smallest acquaintance with the laws of Hebrew poetry . . . These words belong rather to the domain of poetry than history, and this language is that of hyperbole rather than the exact narration of facts (*Pulpit Commentary*, Volume 7, pp. 166,167).

Though couched in poetical language, it is clear from the text that some sign did occur in the heavens. The entire passage is written as a narrative of a miraculous event that actually happened. The question, therefore, is, "What is the nature of that event?"

2.   Eclipse Of The Sun

Some feel the passage refers to an eclipse of the sun. One such person was the great Old Testament scholar, Robert Dick Wilson who translated Joshua 10:12b-14 as follows:

> Be eclipsed, O sun, in Gibeon, and thou moon in the valley of Aijalon!

And the sun was eclipsed and the moon turned back, while the nation was avenged on its enemies. It is not written in the Book of Jasher?

And the sun stayed in the half of the heaven, and set not hastily as when a day is done.

And there was never a day like that day before or since, in respect to Jehovah's hearing the voice of a man.

(Robert Dick Wilson, "What Does 'The Sun Stood Still Mean?' " *Moody Monthly*, October 1920).

According to this view, God granted Joshua's request for a favorable sign by causing an eclipse of the sun.

3. Earth Literally Stopped Rotating

Many have held that the earth actually stopped rotating for about twenty-four hours. From the peoples' vantage point the sun would have *appeared* to have stopped. Though this would give Joshua the time to win the battle, it would also cause terrible catastrophes on the planet. Those who believe in the power of God realize that He could have prevented these catastrophes from occurring.

4. Slower Rotation Of Earth

Some read the text to mean that a retardation of the movement of the earth is what happened. Instead of taking twenty-four hours for one rotation, it took from thirty-six to forty-eight hours. This would have given Joshua and his armies sufficient daylight to win the battle over their enemies without causing the major disturbances that would have happened if the earth stopped rotating. Old Testament authority Gleason Archer writes:

It has been objected that if in fact the earth was stopped for a period of twenty-four hours, inconceivable catastrophe would have befallen the entire planet and everything on its surface. While those who believe in the omnipotence of God would hardly concede that Yahweh could not have prevented such catastrophe and held in abeyance the physical laws that might be brought to pass, it does not seem to be absolutely necessary (on the basis of the Hebrew text itself) to hold that the planet was suddenly halted in its rotation. Verse 13 states that the sun "did not hasten to go down for about a whole day" (NASB). The words "did not hasten" seem to point to a retardation of the movement so that the rotation required forty-eight hours rather than the usual twenty-four (Gleason Archer, *Encyclopedia of Bible Difficulties*, Grand Rapids, Michigan: Zondervan, 1982, p. 161).

Donald K. Campbell concurs:

The best explanation seems to be the view that in answer to Joshua's prayer God caused the rotation of the earth to slow down so that it made one full rotation in 48 hours rather than in 24. It seems apparent that this view is supported by both the poem in verses 12b-13a and the prose in verse 13b (Donald K. Campbell, *The Bible Knowledge Commentary*, John Walvoord and Roy Zuck. eds., Wheaton, Illinois: Victor Books, 1985, p. 351).

God caused the rotation of the earth to slow down. The earth, therefore, made one full rotation around the sun in a longer period of time. This fits with verse 13 which says, "The sun ... delayed going down about a full day." Thus the sun was abnormally slow in getting to sunset, giving Joshua and his soldiers sufficient time to complete their victorious battle.

5.   Miracle Of Refraction

There are some who see this as a miracle of refraction. This theory contends the earth continued to rotate at its normal speed while God supernaturally gave a mirage that made it appear that the sun and the moon were out of their regular place. Thus, God supernaturally provided more daylight so that Joshua could win the battle. This provides Joshua with the necessary light to fight the battle, yet to do so does not force us to accept any change in the rotation of the earth.

6. Stop Moving Or Stop Shining?

Another view is that the prayer of Joshua was not for the prolongation of the day, but rather that the sun would cease pouring down its heat on him and his troops. The prayer was actually for the cessation of light, not its prolongation. God answered by sending a hailstorm that allowed Joshua's weary troops to win the battle. Thus 'stand still' means to keep from shining. E.W. Maunder explains:

> From what was it then that Joshua wished the sun to cease: from its moving or from its shining? It is not possible that, engaged as he was in a desperate battle, he was even so much as thinking of the sun's motion at all. But its shining, its scorching heat, must have been most seriously felt by him. At noon, in high summer, southern Palestine is one of the hottest countries in the world. It is impossible to suppose Joshua wished for the sun to be fixed overhead, where it must have been distressing his men who had already been seventeen hours on foot. A very arduous pursuit lay before them and the enemy must have been fresher than the Israelites. The sun's heat therefore must have been a serious hindrance, and Joshua must have desired it to be tempered. And the Lord hearkened to his voice and gave him this and much more. A great hailstorm swept up from the west, bringing with it a sudden lowering of temperature, and no doubt hiding the sun (E.W. Maunder, *International Standard Bible Encyclopedia*, W. Lotz, M.G. Kyle, C.E. Armerding, eds., Revised edition, Grand Rapids: Wm. B. Eerdmans Publishing Company, 1979, Vol. 1, p. 448).

Thus, the miracle was not a prolonging of the light but rather a cessation of it. Joshua's prayer was not at the end of the day asking for prolonged sunlight, rather it was at high noon asking for relief from the sun. The sun stopped shining in that it became dark. It was the sun that stopped shining, not that the whole solar system was stopped.

7. Night Prolonged

There are those who say that it was not the day that was prolonged but actually the darkness from the previous night. Hugh J. Blair says:

> It has usually been assumed that Joshua prayed for the day to be prolonged. But is it not possible that what Joshua needed even more, since, as is expressly stated in v.9, he came upon the camp of the enemy by night, was that the darkness continue and the night be prolonged for a surprise attack? That it was early morning when he made his request is evident from the position of the moon in the valley of Aijalon (to the west) and the position of the sun over Gibeon (to the east) (v.12). The answer came in a hailstorm which had the effect of prolonging the darkness. (Hugh J. Blair, *New Bible Commentary*, p. 244).

This view would be make it Joshua's long night rather than a long day.

Conclusion

We have seen that there are a variety of explanations to Joshua's long day without having to admit to scientific error. Although several of these views are possible, the theory that the sun actually slowed down its movement seems to be the best way of looking at the evidence. Leon Wood writes:

> The traditional view must be maintained, however, for these alternate explanations do not do justice to the language of the text. Though it is true the verb *dum* (translated 'stand still' in Joshua's call) means basically "be silent" and so could refer to being silent in other ways than retardation of movement, still the verb *amadh* is also used (twice in v. 13) and it definitely indicates a change in pattern of movement. Further, verse 13 closes with the expression "and hasted not to go down," where the word "hasted" (*uz*) again speaks of motion, and the phrase "to go down" (*labho*) is normally in reference to the sun setting. Still further, verse 14 states that this day was unique in

history which suggests a major miracle occurred such as to the prolongation of a natural day. The extent of the prolongation can also be estimated. Since the hour was noon when Joshua voiced the call, and it was stated that the sun did not go down for "about a whole day" (*keyom tamin*), it is likely that the afternoon hours until sunset were prolonged twice their normal length. In other words, the total daylight hours of the day were one and one-half times normal (Leon Wood, *A Survey of Israel's History*, Grand Rapids: Zondervan, 1970, p. 181).

Wood explains how this would have effected the universe:

As to how this was effected, the closing words of vs. 13 "and hasted not to go down about a whole day," suggest that the relative positions of the sun and the earth did not hold still but merely slowed in their change. This means that the earth simply slowed, in its speed of rotation on its axis, approximately to half that of normal. This did not affect the speed of movement around the sun of the rest of the solar system, which complicating factors have been mentioned in criticism by those advocating other explanations (Leon Wood, *A Survey of Israel's History*, p. 181, note 47).

Though this may be the best view, several of the others are certainly possible. Donald H. Madvig writes:

Reverence for God's Word should encourage us to suspend judgment until more evidence is available. In the meantime no single explanation can be made a test of orthodoxy (Donald H. Madvig, "Joshua," *The Expositors Bible Commentary*, p. 304).

There have been stories circulating about reports of a "missing day" in ancient Egyptian, Chinese, and Hindu sources. There is also the story of a Yale astronomer who found that the earth was twenty-four hours out of schedule:

Another professor at Yale, Dr. Totten, suggested the astronomer read the Bible starting at the beginning and going as far as necessary, to see if the Bible could account for the missing time. When he came to the account of the long day of Joshua, the astronomer rechecked the figures and found that at the time of Joshua there were only twenty-three hours and twenty minutes lost. His skepticism justified, he decided that the Bible was not the Word of God because there was a mistake by forty minutes.

Professor Totten showed him that the Bible account does not say twenty-four hours, but rather 'about the space of a whole day.' On reading farther the astronomer found that God, through the prophet Isaiah and in answer to Hezekiah's prayer, promised to add fifteen years to his life (II Kings 20:1-11; Isaiah 38:1-21). To confirm this promise, the shadow of the sundial was turned back ten degrees. Ten degrees on a sundial is forty minutes on the face of a clock. When he found his day of missing time accounted for in the Bible, the astronomer bowed his head in worship of its Author, saying, "Lord, I believe!" (Harry Rimmer, *The Harmony of Science and Scripture*, Grand Rapids: Eerdmans, 1936, p. 33).

It is unfortunate that these often-told stories lack any documentation. Bernard Ramm explains:

There are two other matters that have been urged as evidence for a lengthened day and this material the author has not been able to track down nor confirm to his own satisfaction as to their accuracy or validity. First, there are Egyptian, Chinese, and Hindu reports of a long day . . . Second, there is the claim . . . that it is common knowledge among astronomers that one full day is missing in our astronomical calculations and that Prof. Pickering of the Harvard Observatory traced it back to the time of Joshua. Maunder of Greenwich and Totten of Yale are then supposed to have taken it right back to the time of Joshua, practically to the year and day. Then Totten added to this the 10° of Ahaz' dial to found out the full day. This I have not been able to verify to my own satisfaction (Bernard Ramm, *A Christian View of Science and The Scripture*, Grand Rapids: Eerdmans, 1955, p. 109).

26

DOES THE BIBLE GIVE AN INACCURATE VALUE TO *PI?*

The following Scripture seems to give an inaccurate value for *pi.*

Then he made the Sea of cast bronze, ten cubits from one brim to the other; it was completely round. Its height was five cubits, and a line of thirty cubits measured its circumference (2 Chronicles 4:2).

Some see this three to one ratio as inconsistent with an inerrant Scripture. The true value of *pi* is 3.14159 rather than 3.0. Is this a scientific error?

Two Possible Solutions

There are two basic ways that this problem can be approached without admitting to a scientific error. The first solution sees the writer as speaking in approximate terms. As we have already said, the Bible does not claim to give technical scientific explanations for things, but rather speaks from the viewpoint of an observer. This is the same thing we all do in everyday speech. Therefore, in this instance, the writer is only speaking in approximate terms.

However, there is another solution that has the biblical writer speaking very precisely. Charles Ryrie explains:

> The ten cubit measurement was from brim to brim; that is from the outside edge to the other. But verse 5 states the width of the edge was a handbreath or about 4 inches. So the insider diameter was ten cubits (180 inches) minus two handbreaths (8 inches). Multiplying 172 inches by *pi*, the total is 540 inches, the same circumference given in verse 2. (Charles Ryrie, *Basic Theology*, Wheaton, Illinois: SP Publications, 1986, p. 99).

Whichever solution is adopted, it is clear that one not need assume a scientific error.

27

HOW COULD IRON FLOAT AND WOOD SINK?

One of the events that the Old Testament records which appears unscientific is given in the Book of Second Kings. It is when wood sank and iron floated.

While Elisha and his fellow prophets were building new facilities near the Jordan River, one of the men lost an axehead as he was cutting down a tree. He cried out in dismay because the axehead had been borrowed. The Bible says Elisha then took charge of the situation:

And the man of God said, 'Where did it fall?' And he showed him the place. So he cut off a stick, and threw it in there; and he made the iron float (2 Kings 6:6).

How are we to understand this event? The properties of iron make it sink while the properties in wood cause it to float.

Miracle

This is an excellent example of a biblical miracle in which God performs a sign contrary to the ordinary routine of nature. Certainly this cannot be repeated in a laboratory experiment and observed. It happened only once for a particular purpose.

The purpose of the sign was to encourage the people. Thomas L. Constable comments:

> Certainly this miracle encouraged the group of faithful followers of the Lord that their God really is alive and that He would supernaturally provide for their needs even though many Israelites had turned from the true God to Baal (Thomas L. Constable, *The Bible Knowledge Commentary*, John Walvoord, Roy Zuck, eds., Wheaton, Illinois: Victor Books, 1985, p. 549).

Alternative Explanation

Aramaic scholar George Lamsa thinks the axehead came to the top of the water because Elisha put the stick in its hole. He translates the verse:

> And he cut off a stick and thrust it in there; and it stuck in the hole of the axehead (George Lamsa, translator, *The Holy Bible Translated from Ancient Eastern Manuscripts*, Philadelphia: A. J. Holman Company, 1961, p. 417).

The miracle was then one of divine guidance. When Elisha put the stick into the water it immediately found the axehead.

There is, however, no basis for his translation, therefore, we are not to look for some ordinary natural explanation to explain this occurrence. It was a miracle of God as a sign to his people that He was with them.

28

DID GOD BACK UP THE SUN FOR HEZEKIAH'S SUNDIAL?

During the reign of King Hezekiah, he asked for a confirmatory sign from the prophet Isaiah to verify that all Isaiah had predicted was true. We have the following account:

And Hezekiah said to Isaiah, 'What is the sign that the Lord will heal me, and that I shall go up to the house of the Lord the third day?' Then Isaiah said, 'This is the sign to you from the Lord, that the Lord will do the thing which He has spoken: shall the shadow go forward ten degrees or go backward ten degrees?' And Hezekiah answered, 'It is an easy thing for the shadow to go down ten degrees, no but let the shadow go backward ten degrees.' So Isaiah the prophet cried out to the Lord, and He brought the shadow ten degrees backward, by which it had gone down on the sundial of Ahaz (2 Kings 20:8-11).

And this is the sign to you from the Lord, that the Lord will do this thing which He has spoken: 'Behold, I will bring the shadow on the sundial, which has gone down with the sun on the sundial of Ahaz, ten degrees backward.' So the sun returned ten degrees on the dial by which it had gone down (Isaiah 38:7,8).

Hezekiah was offered a choice: the shadow on the sundial could go either 10 degrees backwards or forwards. Hezekiah assumed that the sun going backward would be a greater sign since it would go against nature. God granted Isaiah's prayer and the sign occurred.

Which Sundial?

How did God move the sundial? Part of our consideration of this miracle concerns the type of sundial that was in mind. There have been three different suggestions:

1. The sundial was possibly a series of steps leading from east to west. As the sun sank in the west the shadow would come down the steps and a glance at this shadow on the steps would indicate how much daytime was left.

2. Another type suggested is a hollowed out hemisphere with lines on the inside wherein the shaded part will intersect various lines and show the time of day.

3. A third suggestion is that the sundial was a pillar with steps around it and as the sun moved across the heavens, the shadow of the pillar would fall on different steps, thus, giving a rough estimate of the time of day.

Regardless which of the three sundials were used the miracle would be obvious to all concerned. It would not be as miraculous for the shadow to advance ten degrees as for the shadow to retreat. Only supernatural intervention could cause the latter. This is the miracle that Hezekiah received. If the miracle occurred, how and what happened?

Sun Backed Up?

One possibility is that the earth backed up in its trajectory to shed more daylight upon the sundial. The problem with this view is that it disturbs all the machinery in the heavens. There would have been untold destruction if this happened unless God supernaturally intervened. While this is possible, it is not necessary to assume that this is what occurred.

In addition, 2 Chronicles 32:31 seems to restrict the phenomenon to the land of Palestine:

However, regarding the ambassadors of the princes of Babylon, whom they sent to inquire about the wonder that was done in the land, God withdrew from him, in order to test him, that He might know all that was in his heart (2 Chronicles 32:31).

If this be the case, then it is not necessary to say that the sun backed up its trajectory.

Mirage

Others have thought that the miracle was a supernatural mirage of the sun:

The theory of Butler is that the miracle was a 'supernatural superior mirage of the sun.' Lateral images have been known to shift objects ninety degrees. Butler tells of Martin, one of the round-the-world fliers of 1924, who crashed his plane in Alaska because a lateral image moved a mountain ninety degrees out of its place! So, Butler reasons, a superior image of ten degrees would be no great phenomenon (Bernard Ramm, *The Christian View Of Science and Scripture*, Grand Rapids: Eerdmans, 1954, p. 111).

Lighting Up The Steps

The miracle was more likely that of lighting up the steps. This is a result of the direct intervention of God. W.F. Arndt comments:

The writer does not say that this was due to the movement of the sun. He furnishes no explanation. His account makes it possible to assume that the miracle was confined to what happened on the sundial . . . The prominence which is given to the dial and the shadow strongly supports this view. Since there is no mention of the lengthening of the day, this seems preferable to the view that understands Isaiah to say that the sun reversed its course and shone ten hours or so longer than usually (W.F. Arndt, *Bible Difficulties*, St. Louis: Concordia Publishers, p. 126).

Conclusion

We conclude that God performed a supernatural sign for King Hezekiah by making the shadow on the sundial retreat. There are several possible ways how he could have done it and we cannot be sure which, if any, of the suggested ways were used. The fact is that God did grant Hezekiah this sign.

Attempts to explain this scientifically or to relate it to some calendrical adjustment—perhaps in conjuction with Joshua's long day (Josh. 10)—have not carried full conviction with students of science or chronology. It is best to admit that we do not know the explanation but to accept the testimony of the word of God to the fact a miracle took place (Geoffrey W. Grogan, Isaiah, *The Expositors Bible Commentary*, Vol. 6, Frank E. Gabelein, General editor, Grand Rapids Mi: Zondervan, 1986, p. 236).

29

WAS JONAH SWALLOWED BY A WHALE?

There have been a number of accounts in Scripture that have caused problems for scientists and non-scientists alike. One of the more prominent accounts is the story of Jonah and the whale:

Now the Lord prepared a great fish to swallow Jonah. And Jonah was in the belly of the fish three days and three nights (Jonah 1:17).

Are we to understand this literally? Was Jonah actually swallowed by a large fish?

Not Necessarily A Whale

To begin with we must note that the Hebrew word does not necessarily correspond to our modern designation whale. It simply means a large sea creature and could refer to anything found in the sea. Old Testament authority Gleason Archer writes:

Incidentally, it should be observed that the Hebrew text of Jonah 2:1 actually reads *dag gadol*, or "great fish" rather than a technical term for "whale." But since Hebrew possessed no special word for "whale," and since no true fish—as opposed to a marine mammal—is known to possess a stomach as capacious as a whale's, it is reasonable to adhere to the traditional interpretation at this point. The only other available term, *tannin*, was too vague to be serviceable here, since it could also mean shark, sea serpent, or even dragon (Gleason Archer, Jr., *A Survey of Old Testament Introduction*, Revised edition, Chicago: Moody Press, 1974, p. 314).

Did then a large sea creature literally swallow Jonah?

History Or Fiction?

Many people view the Book of Jonah as unhistorical and unscientific:

Many Jews and Christians, in spite of the difficulties, have accepted the story as history. In the pre-scientific era this literal interpretation was acceptable (Madeleine S. Miller and J. Lane Miller, Jonah, *Harper's Bible Dictionary*, New York: Harper and Row, 1952, p. 345).

The Book of Jonah treats the account as history, not allegory. Furthermore, there is every good reason to accept this as a historical record. This can be seen by observing the following:

1.   Jonah was a historical character.

2.   The book was written as historical narrative.

3.   The traditional view of Jews and Christians is that the book is historical.

4.   Jesus testified to the book's historicity.

Jonah Existed

We know from another biblical reference that there was a prophet to Israel named Jonah:

He restored the territory of Israel from the entrance of Hamath to the Sea of the Arabah, according to the word of the Lord God of Israel, which He had spoken through his servant Jonah the son of Amittai, the prophet who was from Gath Hepher (2 Kings 14:25).

Historical Narrative

The Book of Jonah is written as a historical narrative. There is no indication within the account that it is to be treated otherwise. Until recently, neither Christians or Jews questioned the historicity of the Book of Jonah. It has been accepted as an account of what actually occurred during the life of the prophet Jonah.

Jesus and Jonah

The historicity of the account of Jonah is confirmed by Jesus Christ. Jesus told the religious leaders of His day that the sign of Jonah was going to be *the* sign of his resurrection:

An evil and adulterous generation seeks after a sign, and no sign will be given to it except the sign of the prophet Jonah. For as Jonah was three days and three nights in the belly of the great fish, so will the Son of Man be three days and three nights in the heart of the earth (Matthew 12:39,40).

Jesus accepted, at face value, the account of Jonah surviving after being swallowed by the sea creature. In His mind the event did literally occur. He also believed the repentance of the people of Nineveh as something that occurred. If Jesus is the One whom He claimed to be, God in human flesh, then His Word settles the matter.

In addition, Jesus puts the historicity of the account of Jonah and the fish on the same level as His resurrection. The analogy is clear. As Jonah was so Jesus will be. The Bible teaches that Jesus was literally dead and then resurrected from the dead. The resurrection of Christ is treated as a historical fact as is the account of Jonah.

All things point to the event as having literally occurred.

Not Impossible

The next point that needs to be made is that there are creatures living in the sea which are capable of swallowing a human being whole. Sperm whales have been known to swallow unusually large objects, including a fifteen-foot long shark! (for documentation see Frank T. Bullen, *Cruise of the Cachalot Round the World After Sperm Whales*, London: Smith, 1898). The whale shark, as well as the blue whale, also has the capacity of swallowing a man whole. Sperm whales and whale sharks are not unknown in that part of the world.

Furthermore, Jonah-like incidents have been known to occur. There have been at least two documented reports where men have been swallowed by large sea creatures and have lived through the experience.

One man, Marshall Jenkins, was swallowed alive by a sperm whale in 1771 and survived. Another incident concerns James Bartley. In 1891, Bartley was swallowed by a sperm whale that his whaling crew had harpooned. The whale slipped away, was found and killed a day or so later. Bartley was found alive, but unconscious, in the stomach of the whale. He was revived and in a few weeks regained his health (for documentation see Ambrose James Wilson, *Princeton Theological Revue*, October, 1928). Thus, the account of Jonah cannot be rejected on the basis that:

(1) No such sea creature exists that could swallow a man whole.

(2) The incident is outside the realm of human experience.

However, beyond the fact that a natural explanation could explain the episode is that the Bible says *God* prepared a fish to swallow Jonah. This could mean a special fish made for this very occasion or it could mean that God directed one of the large sea creatures to swallow the wayward prophet. Whatever the case, the supernatural hand of God was involved.

Conclusion

There is every good reason to accept the account of Jonah in a literal manner. The fish involved could have been specially prepared by God or it could have been one of the sea creatures known to be able to swallow a human. Whatever the explanation, the account given in Scripture is miraculous.

30

WHAT WAS THE STAR
OF BETHLEHEM?

The Bible records that a star led the wise men to Jerusalem at the birth of Christ:

> Now after Jesus was born in Bethlehem of Judea in the days of Herod the king, behold, wise men from the East came to Jerusalem, saying, 'Where is He who has been born King of the Jews? For we have seen His star in the East and have come to worship Him' . . . When they heard the king, they departed; and behold the star which they had seen in the East went before them, till it came and stood over where the young child was (Matthew 2:1-2,9).

From this, we see that it was a star in the heavens that led the magi from the East to Jerusalem. From Jerusalem the star then appeared over the place where the child Jesus was. What was this star? Was it sent from God? What was its origin?

Supernova

Some have held the star to be a supernova. A supernova is a star that violently explodes and then proceeds to give off great amounts of light for a short period of time (a few weeks to a few months). But this is only a theory with no evidence to support it. Moreover this theory seems difficult to accept in light of Matthew 2:9 which says the star stood over the place where Jesus was.

Halley's Comet

Others have speculated that it was a comet that passed overhead at that time. Halley's Comet has been suggested as a possibility. But the time of its occurrence, 12 B.C., is too early for the birth of Christ. Furthermore, a comet would not explain Matthew 2:9.

Planetary Conjunction

Another theory holds that what the magi saw was a conjunction of planets. In 7 B.C. in the months of May, October and November, there was a conjunction of the planets Jupiter and Saturn in the zodiacal constellation of Pisces. We know that Jews living during the Middle Ages considered this planetary alignment to have Messianic significance. This could explain many details. If the magi saw the conjunction in May, the later alignments in October and November could explain Matthew 2:9.

The problem with this view is that there is no solid evidence that the ancients referred to such an alignment as a "star." Furthermore, Jupiter and Saturn would have been one degree apart and not fused into the same image. Yet this theory is still a possible explanation of what occurred.

Supernatural Explanation

There are many who believe that the account as given in the Gospel of Matthew demands a purely supernatural interpretation. This would end the need for attempting to find an astronomical explanation of what the magi saw. God may have supernaturally provided the star in the East and then again over the house where the baby Jesus slept. Although the text does not necessarily demand that we take this position, it is entirely possible that we are dealing with a supernatural event that does not find any explanation in the history of astronomy.

Because the evidence is inconclusive we cannot be certain what it was that the magi saw or whether or not it was a supernatural phenomenon. We can, however, be certain that they saw something that was used by God to lead them to Bethlehem and the baby Jesus.

Summary To Section Four

We have seen that the difficulties in the Bible regarding science can all be explained without resorting to labeling the Bible as unscientific.

The Scriptures were written to convey God's revelation of Himself to mankind. In doing so the Bible speaks of things pertaining to science in everyday language. The non-technical language of the Bible should not be used to condemn it as being anti-scientific.

The Bible is often portrayed as being ignorant in the areas of science and nature with statements that contradict known scientific facts. However, this is not the case.

In our next section we shall see that the Bible actually foresees science in advance. It proves to be well ahead of science and scientific discoveries in a variety of fields. The Bible recognizes basic facts of science that were unknown to the rest of the world at that time. This is another indication that it is what it claims to be—the Word of God.

The Bible And Science: Not In Conflict

Jesus said: "You are greatly mistaken, not knowing
the Scriptures nor the power of God."
(Matthew 22:29)

31

DOES THE BIBLE FORESEE
SCIENTIFIC DISCOVERIES?

The Bible does not contain statements that are scientifically inaccurate. They do not make the same absurd mistakes that were made by others living in their day. But the Bible goes further in that it foresees scientific discoveries before they were known to the world at large.

During the time the Bible was being composed there was much superstition and ignorance concerning the nature and function of the the universe. Though no nation or sacred writings were immune to superstition, the Bible is a notable exception. We do not find the biblical writers committing the same types of errors as their contemporaries. Kenny Barfield writes:

We might well wonder if there could be among all the so-called revelations of the world's religions one document that is untouched by the foibles and fallacies of men, one record that reveals an accurate understanding of man and nature, one collection of writings that holds an immutable relationship to scientific truth? One book—and only one—can meet these qualifications. It is known as the Bible . . . .

There is no evidence that any one group of people is inherently more or less intelligent than another. It should also be noted that various cultures have made important progress in the sciences. This progress is understandable on the basis of human genius, equally present in all peoples. Interestingly, within this equality of people is an amazing disparity in certain "sacred writings." The disparity should not be there. But it is (Kenny Barfield, *Why The Bible is Number 1*, Grand Rapids: Baker Book House, 1988, pp. 9,10).

Errors Avoided

Barfield notes some of the the scientific errors avoided by the biblical writers:

Medical Errors Avoided

1. Bizarre prescriptions
2. Attributing all disease to demons
3. Magical control of disease
4. Doctrine of signatures
5. Alchemy
6. Astrology
7. Divination and Omens

Astronomical Errors Avoided

1. Incorrect understanding of the sun and moon
2. Deification of the natural universe
3. A flat earth
4. Incorrect understanding of the size of the universe
5. Astrology
6. A limited number of stars
7. Geocentricity
8. Magic and omens

Earth Science Errors Avoided

1. Belief in a living earth
2. Deification of nature
3. Astrological influences regarding nature
4. Magical control of nature
5. Demonological influence of nature

6. Incorrect understanding of earthquakes, storms, oceans, mountains, lightning, and other physical phenomenon

(Kenny Barfield, *Why The Bible is Number 1*, pp. 40,130,163).

Science Foreseen

The biblical writers not only avoided scientific errors, they also were able to foresee scientific discoveries years ahead of their time. The following examples should demonstrate that the biblical writers were given information that their contemporaries did not have.

Earth Not Supported

The Scripture also says that the earth hangs in space:

He stretches out the north over empty space; He hangs the earth on nothing (Job 26:7).

This idea was an oddity in the ancient world, for most people believed the earth was supported by something.

Stars Innumerable

The Bible also speaks of innumerable stars:

As the host of heaven cannot be numbered, nor the sand of the sea measured (Jeremiah 33:22).

Before the telescope was invented, people believed they could count the stars. Even the great astronomer Johann Kepler numbered the stars at slightly over one thousand. Not until modern times did man realize that numbering the stars is an impossibility.

Circularity Of The Earth

The Bible speaks of the circularity of the earth:

It is He who sits above the circle of the earth (Isaiah 40:22).

Early man usually viewed the earth as being flat.

Dietary Regulations

The Israelites were forbidden to eat the flesh of any animal that had died a natural death:

You shall not eat anything that dies of itself (Deuteronomy 14:21).

Today we know that dead animals can carry lice, flies, and fleas. Each of these are carriers of disease.

Quarantine Of Contagious Diseases

God ordered those who had contagious diseases to be separated from the rest of the camp:

Now the leper on whom the sore is, his clothes shall be torn and his head bare; and he shall cover his mustache, and cry, 'Unclean! Unclean!' He shall be unclean. All the days he has the sore he shall be unclean. He is unclean, and he shall dwell alone; his habitation shall be outside the camp (Leviticus 13:45,46).

The Bible is the only book in the ancient world that ordered this practice.

Water Supply

The children of Israel were forbidden to drink water from small or stagnant pools or from water that had been contaminated by coming into contact with animals or meat (Leviticus 11:29-36). It is only in the last 100 years that medical science has learned that contaminated water can cause typhoid and cholera.

Rabbits And Pork

Today humans eat rabbits and pork, although both are susceptible to infectious parasites. The children of Israel were not allowed to eat either of these animals. Though they may be cleanly fed and well-cooked, they both can be a source of disease. Roasting pork over an open flame is not sufficient to kill the parasites that could have attached themselves to the animal. Parasites can also be transmitted by the mere handling of pork. Consequently, the children of Israel were not even allowed to touch the body of a dead swine.

Hygienic Regulations

The Bible contains hygienic regulations for the children of Israel. The Bible commands that sewage should be disposed of outside the camp of Israel:

> Also you shall have a place outside the camp, where you may go out; and you shall have an implement among your equipment, and when you sit down outside, you shall dig with it and turn and cover your refuse (Deuteronomy 23:12,13).

This precaution would help eliminate diseases such as typhoid fever.

Circumcision On The Eighth Day

God also commanded his people to circumcise the male children on the eighth day:

> He who is eight days old among you shall be circumcised, every male child in your generations (Genesis 17:12).

The full meaning of that command has only been recently understood. Doctor Russel J. Thomsen writes:

> One simple aspect of God's command to Abraham helped prevent excessive bleeding with circumcision of the

newborn. That was the instruction that the rite should be done on the eighth day of life. Modern medicine has come to understand the mechanisms at work in the clotting of blood. Of major importance in blood clotting is prothrombin, a compound made in the liver and the precursor of the active clotting agent thrombin. It has been well established that within a few hours after birth prothrombin becomes relatively depleted and does not become replenished by the infant's liver until about the eighth day of life (Russel J. Thomsen, M.D., *Medical Wisdom From the Bible*, Old Tappan, New Jersey: Fleming H. Revell Company, 1974, p. 17).

It has been only since 1940 that it has become a standard practice to circumcise all male infants.

Pest Control

The Bible also gave a prescription for the control of pests. Robert Boyd writes:

A sure-fire remedy for the control of pests was given centuries ago, and yet we are plagued today with insects, oftimes with no remedy. Moses commanded Israel to set aside one year in seven when no crops were raised [Leviticus] 25:1-24 . God promised sufficient harvest in the sixth year to provide for this period. Following this plan, here's what would happen—insects winter in the stalks of the last year's harvest, hatch in the spring, and are perpetuated by laying eggs in the new crop. Now, if one year in seven no crop were raised, there is nothing for the insects to subsist upon and the pests are controlled by this method. Man's method today is crop rotation, but we're still pestered with insects. This method will never approach God's method. "Then there was the year of Jubilee after every seven Sabbatical years, which would serve to eliminate the insects which had a cycle of seven years or more or less and which were not affected by the one year in seven" (Robert Boyd, *Boyd's Bible Handbook*, Eugene, Oregon: Harvest House Publishers, 1983, p. 78).

Many other examples could be added. With regard to science, the biblical writers were separate from their contemporaries in the ancient world in the following two ways: (1) they did not repeat the commonly held errors of their day (2) they spoke of things that only present-day science has come to realize is scientifically accurate.

Be Careful Of Extremes

While we believe that the Scriptures are scientifically accurate and that there are some examples of Scripture foreseeing modern science, there are some writers who have gone too far in their assertion that the Bible anticipates modern science. R.M. Page writes:

> Some writers, notably Rimmer, Sanden and Beirnes, have found Scriptural passages in which they see anticipations of modern scientific discovery. The undalatory theory of matter is seen in Genesis 1:2. Wireless telegraph is seen in Job 38:35. The concept of parallax is seen in James 1:17. Atomic theory of matter is seen in Hebrews 11:3 and atomic binding in Hebrews 1:3. Light as the basis of all substance is seen in Genesis 1:3, nuclear fission in Genesis 1:4, and a final chain reaction in Isaiah 34:4 and Luke 21:25-28. An expanding universe is seen in Isaiah 40:22. Motor cars are seen in Joel 2:3,4, airplanes in Isaiah 31:5 and 60:8, and submarines in Revelation 11:3-12 (R.M. Page, "Science in the Bible," *The Zondervan Pictorial Encyclopedia of the Bible*, Merril C. Tenney, General editor, Volume 5, Grand Rapids: Zondervan, 1977, p. 295).

Summary And Conclusion

The fact that the Bible foresees modern science is another evidence of its divine inspiration. How else can we explain the references to scientific matters that were done years ahead of their time? Furthermore, why didn't the biblical writers repeat the common unscientific errors of their day? The answer is simple. The writings of Scripture were inspired by the Creator Himself.

32

WHAT ANSWERS DOES THE BIBLE HAVE FOR A NON-BELIEVING WORLD?

We now come to our final question in our study of the subject of the Bible and science. What answers does the Bible have to offer to a non-believing world? We again emphasize that unbelieving science has no ultimate answers to questions of the origin and meaning of life. Concerning the origin of the universe, Robert Jastrow wrote:

Now we would like to pursue that inquiry further back in time, but the barrier to further progress seems insurmountable. It is not a matter of another year, another decade of work, another measurement, another theory; at this moment it seems as though science will never be able to raise the curtain on the mystery of creation. For the scientist who has lived by his faith in the power of reason, the story ends like a bad dream. He has scaled the mountains of ignorance; he is able to conquer the highest peak; as he pulls himself over the final rock, he is greeted by a band of theologians who have been sitting there for centuries (Robert Jastrow, *God and the Astronomers*, New York: W.W. Norton and Company, Inc., 1978, p. 113).

Admission Of Unbelieving Scientists

Many unbelieving scientists will admit there is evidence for a Creator. One scientist wrote:

> The world is too complicated in all its parts and interconnections to be due to chance alone. I am convinced that the existence of life with all its order in each of its organisms is simply too well put together. Each part of a living thing depends on all its other parts to function. How does each part know? How is each part specified at conception? The more one learns about biochemistry the more unbelievable it becomes unless there is some type of organizing principle—an architect (Allan Sandage, *Truth*, Vol. 1, Dallas: Texas, Truth Incorporated, 1985, p. 54).

Michael Denton explains the complexity of a simple cell:

> To grasp the reality of life as it has been revealed by molecular biology, we must magnify a cell a thousand million times until it is twenty kilometers in diameter and resembles a giant airship large enough to cover a great city like London or New York. What we would then see would be an object of unparalleled complexity and adaptive design. On the surface of the cell we would see millions of openings, like the port holes of a vast space ship, opening and closing to allow a continual stream of materials to flow in and out. If we were to enter one of those openings we would then find ourselves in a world of supreme technology and bewildering complexity. . . .
>
> Is it really credible that random processes could have constructed a reality, the smallest element of which—a functional protein or gene—is complex beyond our our own creative capacities, a reality which is the very antithesis of chance, which excels in every sense anything produced by the intelligence of man? (Michael Denton, *Evolution: A Theory in Crisis*, Bethesda, Maryland: Adler and Adler, 1985, pp. 328,342).

After examining the evidence for the creationist view scientist Michael Pitman concluded:

I started as devil's advocate for the creationist view and came, in principle, though not according to any particular creed, to prefer it . . . For this it will probably be condemned from some quarters. But I hope I have shown that apparently convincing arguments in support of a belief can often be seen to be either based on insufficient data or open to more than one interpretation; and that much that passes for science is no more and no less emotional, illogical and idiosyncratic than many of the opposing arguments . . . .

Adam and Evolution should be controversial. The many issues it raises cannot all be dealt with, let alone in depth, in a single sweep. But the direction of the argument is clear—there has been neither chemical evolution nor macro-evolution. Nor as some twentieth century churchmen bio-illogically accept, did God involve chance mutations in 'creation by evolution'. No intelligent creator would leave matters to chance; on the contrary his purpose would be to realize, in plan and practice, his ideas. Pressing the logic to its conclusion, this book advocates a grand and full-blooded creation. The implications of this view necessitate a reappraisal of ourselves and of the whole world of organisms around us (Michael Pitman, *Adam and Evolution*, Grand Rapids: Baker Book House, 1987, pp. 254, 255).

Though neither the evolutionary model or the creation model can be proven scientifically, we have seen that the evidence supports special creation. There is no need to be ashamed of holding to a belief in God as Creator. Though the person who believes in creation may not have every answer to questions of evolutionary scientists, he does have sufficient answers. If one wishes to put his faith in the God of the Bible he can do so with intelligent faith that is based upon the best available evidence. No one has to "assassinate his brains" to be a believer in the God of the Bible.

A Final Thought

We have seen that the evidence, both biblical and scientific, points to a Creator who is the God of the Bible. This being the case we can make the following conclusions:

God Does Exist

The existence of God is clear from both biblical and scientific evidence. The world around us testifies to the existence, power and love of God. The Bible says:

The heavens declare the glory of God and the firmament shows His handiwork (Psalm 19:1).

God Has Spoken

The Bible says that God exists and has spoken to us. Without divine revelation we would not know the difference between ourselves and animals. Fortunately, God has given us the answers in His Word.

Life Has Purpose

Instead of life being meaningless, we now discover there is a purpose for our existence. We can have a relationship with the true and living God through His Son Jesus Christ.

Salvation Has Been Provided

The separation from the presence of God that sin has caused has been overcome by the death of Jesus Christ on the crosss. He has provided salvation and eternal life to those who put their trust in Him.

There Is Hope For The Future

The Bible provides genuine hope for the future. Because Christ died and rose again, we all have hope for a life beyond the grave. For the believer, death leads to glory.

God's Questions To Man

Astronomer Carl Sagan is famous for making the statement, "The cosmos is all there was, is or ever will be."

This is a statement of faith. The Bible records questions that God has given to scientists like Sagan who make such assertions:

Where were you when I laid the foundations of the earth? Tell Me if you have understanding. Who determined its measurements? Surely you know! Or who stretched the line upon it? To what were its foundations fastened? Or who laid its cornerstone? (Job 38:4-6).

In a similar vein Jesus asked:

If I have told you earthly things and you do not believe, how will you believe if I tell you heavenly things? (John 3:12).

It is clear that the only reliable answers concerning the meaning of our existence are found in the Bible. The Creator of the universe has revealed Himself in Scripture so that the entire world may know who He is and what He expects from them.

A final question we leave with the reader is simple: Do you know Him personally?

Recommended Reading

The following books are recommended for further reading in the Bible/science debate. Unfortunately, some of these books are now out of print. They can usually be found in libraries of Christian colleges.

Andrews, E.H. *From Nothing to Nature*. Durham, England: Evangelical Press, 1978.

_____ *God, Science and Evolution*. Welwyn, Herts, England: Evangelical Press, 1980.

Barfield, Kenny. *Why the Bible is Number 1*. Grand Rapids, Michigan: Baker Book House, 1988.

Bird, Wendell. *The Origin of the Species Revisited*. Volumes 1 & 2, New York: Philosophical Library, 1988.

Brown, Walter. *In The Beginning*, Phoenix, Arizona: Center for Scientific Creation, 1989.

Cameron, Nigel. *Evolution and the Authority of the Bible*. Exeter, England: Paternoster Press, 1983.

Chittick, Donald. *The Controversy*. Portland, Oregon: Multnomah Press, 1983.

Davidheiser, Bolton. *Evolution and the Christian Faith*. Phillipsburg, NJ: Presbyterian and Reformed Publishing Company, 1969.

Denton, Michael. *Evolution: A Theory in Crisis*. Bethesda, Maryland: Adler and Adler, 1986.

Dillow, Joseph. *The Waters Above*. Chicago: Moody Press, 1981.

Dolphin, Lambert. *Jesus: Lord of Space and Time.* Green Forest Arizona: New Leaf Press, 1988.

Fix, William. *The Bone Peddlers: Selling Evolution.* New York: MacMillan, 1984.

Gange, Robert. *Origins and Destiny.* Dallas: Word Publishing, 1986.

Gish, Duane. *Evolution: The Challenge of the Fossil Record.* El Cajon, California: Master Books, 1985.

Hitching, Francis. *The Neck of the Giraffe.* London: Pan Publishing, 1982.

Johnson, Phillip E. *Darwin on Trial.* Downers Grove, Illinois: InterVarsity Press, 1991.

Keane, G.J. *Creation Rediscovered.* Doncaster, Victoria, Australia: Credis Pty. Ltd. 1991.

Klotz, John. *Studies in Creation.* St. Louis: Concordia Press, 1985.

Lerner, Eric. *The Big Bang Never Happened.* New York, Times Books: Random House, 1991.

MacBeth, Norman. *Darwin Retried: An Appeal to Reason.* Ipswich, Ma.: Gambit Publishers, 1971.

Morris, Henry and Gary Parker. *What is Creation Science?* El Cajon, Calif.: Master Books, 1982.

Pitman, Michael. *Adam and Evolution.* Grand Rapids, Michigan: Baker Book House, 1987.

Ramm, Bernard. *The Christian View of Science and Scripture.* Grand Rapids, Michigan: Eerdmans, 1954.

Rosevear, David. *Creation Science.* Chichester, England: New Wine Press, 1991.

Schaeffer, Francis A. *Genesis in Space and Time*. Downers Grove, Illinois: InterVarsity Press, 1972.

Stewart, Don. *Understanding the Early Chapters of Genesis*. Spokane, Washington: AusAmerica Publishers, 1993.

Sunderland, Luther. *Darwin's Enigma*. Santee, California: Master Books, 1988.

Taylor, Charles. *The Oldest Science Book in the World*. Queensland, Australia: Assembly Press Pty. Ltd., 1984.

Taylor, Ian. *In the Minds of Men*. Revised Edition, Toronto, Canada: TFE Publishing, 1987.

Thaxton, Charles, Bradley, Walter, Olsen, Roger. *The Mystery of Life's Origin: Reassessing Current Theories*. New York: Philosophical Library, 1984.

Whitcomb, John. *The Early Earth*. Grand Rapids, Michigan: Baker Book House, Revised edition, 1972.

_____ *The World That Perished*. Grand Rapids, Michigan: Baker Book House, Second edition, 1988.

Wilder-Smith, A.E. *Man's Origin, Man's Destiny*. Minneapolis: Bethany Fellowship, 1975.

Wysong, Randy. *The Creation-Evolution Controversy*. Midland, Michigan: Inquiry Press, 1976.

Youngblood, Ronald. (editor) *The Genesis Debate*. Nashville: Thomas Nelson Publishers, 1986.

ABOUT THE AUTHOR

Don Stewart is one of the most successful writers in the country, having authored or co-authored over thirty books. These include *In Search of the Lost Ark: The Quest for the Ark of the Covenant, You Be The Judge: Is Christianity True,* and *10 Reasons To Trust the Bible.*

His writings have also achieved international success. Twenty-seven of his titles have been translated into different languages, including Chinese, Finnish, Polish, Spanish, German, and Portuguese.

Don received his undergraduate degree at Biola University majoring in Bible. He received a masters degree from Talbot Theological Seminary, graduating with the highest honors. Don is a member of the national honor society, Kappa Tau Epsilon.

Don is also an internationally-known apologist, a defender of the historic Christian faith. In his defense of Christianity he has traveled to over thirty countries, speaking at colleges, universities, churches, seminars, and retreats. His topics include the evidence for Christianity, the identity of Jesus Christ, the challenge of the cults, and the relationship of the Bible and science.

Because of his international success as an author and speaker, Don's books have generated sales of over one million copies.

OTHER BOOKS AVAILABLE BY DON STEWART

The following titles from Don Stewart are presently available from AusAmerica Publishers, formerly Dart Press.

What Everyone Needs To Know About God	$9.95
What Everyone Needs To Know About Jesus	$9.95
What Everyone Needs To Know About The Holy Spirit	$9.95
What Everyone Needs To Know About The Bible	$9.95
The Coming Temple:	
Center Stage for the Final Countdown	$9.95
In Search of the Lost Ark: The Quest for	
the Ark of the Covenant	$11.95
10 Reasons to Trust the Bible	$6.95
You Be The Judge: Is Christianity True?	$3.95

AusAmerica Publishers
Box 28010
Spokane, Washington 99228-8010

Washington state residents, add 8% sales tax

Shipping/Handling $2.00

You may also order by credit card by calling toll free
1-800-637-5177 from 9 a.m. to 5 p.m. Monday through Friday
Pacific Standard Time.